Workbook

MORE! 2

Gerngross · Puchta · Holzmann
Stranks · Lewis-Jones

W0397849

hoonzel 1A

HELBLING
LANGUAGES

Mit Bescheid vom 4. Oktober 2007, GZ: BMUKK-5.000/52-V/9/2006, hat das Bundesministerium für Unterricht, Kunst und Kultur das Unterrichtsmittel „MORE! Workbook 2" von Gerngross u.a. antragsgemäß in der vorliegenden Fassung gemäß §14 Abs. 2 und 5 des Schulunterrichtsgesetzes, BGBl. Nr. 472/86 und gemäß den derzeit geltenden Lehrplänen als für den Unterrichtsgebrauch an Hauptschulen und an allgemein bildenden höheren Schulen für die Klasse 2 im Unterrichtsgegenstand Englisch (1. lebende Fremdsprache) geeignet erklärt.

Zeichenerklärung

● leichte Aufgabenstellung

■ Aufgabenstellung mittleren Schwierigkeitsgrades

★ anspruchsvolle Aufgabenstellung

▶ SB p. 15 Diese Übungen passen zur angegebenen Seite im Student's Book.

(1) Diese Übung gehört zum Kernstoff und sollte nicht ausgelassen werden.

(2) Diese Übung kann bei Zeitmangel im Sinne eines "Fast track" durch die Unit ohne Probleme ausgelassen werden.

MORE! WORKBOOK 2
by Günter Gerngross, Herbert Puchta, Christian Holzmann, Jeff Stranks, Peter Lewis-Jones

Edited by Ros Cantalamessa, Oonagh Wade, Johanna Günther
Design and layout by Amanda Hockin
Illustrated by Svjetlan Junaković, Roberto Battestini, Francesca Carabelli, Sergio Cingolaniti, Björn Pertoft, Giovanni Rolandi, Lorenzo Sabbatini

Printed by Athesia

First published 2008

Second edition 2009, sixth print run 2014

ISBN 978-3-85272-050-0

Schulbuchnummer: 135.561
© Helbling Languages 2008
www.helblinglanguages.at

This publication is in copyright.
All rights reserved; no part of this publication may be reproduced, stored in a retrieval system, or transmitted in any form or by any means, electronic, mechanical, photocopying, recording, or otherwise, without the prior written permission of the Publishers.

Contents

UNIT 1 Welcome back

● **1 Write the days of the week in the correct places.**

Friday ~~Monday~~ Saturday Wednesday
Tuesday Thursday ~~Sunday~~

Monday	....
....	....
....	Sunday
....	

● **2 Find the correct answers. Write the numbers in the boxes.**

1 What does Jessica usually do on Fridays after school?

3 Where does she usually go on Saturdays?

2 What does she usually do on Sunday mornings?

4 Does she often do homework on Saturdays and Sundays?

☐ She goes to her friend's place.
☐ Yes, she does.
☐ She goes for a long walk with her dog.
☐ She goes skating with friends.

■ **3 Write the words in the correct order to make questions.**

1 Saturdays? / you / go / on / to / Do / school

....

2 do / Monday evenings? / What / usually / you / do / on

....

3 watch / television / Fridays? / you / on / Do

....

4 usually / Where / go / you / do / Saturday afternoons? / on

....

● **4 Write answers.**

1 Does Matthew play football on Friday afternoons? (✓) Yes, he does.
2 Does Matthew sleep on Sunday mornings? (✗) ....
3 Does Matthew often go to the cinema on Wednesday afternoons? (✓) ....
4 Does Matthew go to school on Saturday mornings? (✗) ....
5 Does Matthew play in a band on Monday afternoons? (✓) ....
6 Does Matthew always watch the sports programme on Monday evenings? (✓) ....

▶ SB p. 10

- **5** **Read the texts and circle T (*True*) or F (*False*).**

Fatih (Turkey): Hi, my name's Fatih. I'm twelve and I've got two sisters and two brothers. I live in a village about 50 kilometres from Istanbul. My favourite food is Lahmacun. It's like pizza. I like video games and nature programmes. I also play football and I swim a lot. With my pocket money (it's not much) I buy sweets. I don't have a pet, because my mum doesn't like animals.

Clare (Scotland): Hi, I'm Clare. I live in Dundee in Scotland. I'm twelve. I've got one brother. He's 21 and he works in Edinburgh. My favourite food is chicken. And I also like chocolate a lot. My friend Moira and I often go to the park (we're skateboarders) and in the evenings we watch TV together. We like sitcoms best. I also like reading (Moira doesn't, she doesn't want to read the Harry Potter books) and horse riding. I've got two pets – a cat and a guinea pig.

Justyna (Poland): Hi, I'm Justyna. I live in Krakow and I've got two little brothers. I'm thirteen and my brothers are five and eight. My favourite food is fish, but we don't eat it very often. I play handball in our school team and I'm also in the swimming team. I love going to the cinema. A lot of films are in English. That's good for me. I can listen to English a lot. I buy magazines with my pocket money. I haven't got a pet.

Sean (Ireland): Hi, I'm Sean, I'm from Sligo in Ireland. I live on a farm and I really like animals. We've got lots of animals, but I don't have a real pet. We've got six horses and I really like horse riding. My friends and I also play football and computer games. I often help at home. My dad gives me some pocket money for that. I buy computer games with the money. My favourite food is pizza.

1. Fatih has got two sisters and a brother. T / F
2. Fatih lives in Istanbul. T / F
3. Fatih's favourite food is Lahmacun. T / F
4. Clare's favourite food is chicken. T / F
5. Clare loves sitcoms. T / F
6. Clare's got one pet. T / F
7. Justyna plays handball and basketball. T / F
8. Justyna loves going to the cinema. T / F
9. Justyna hasn't got a pet. T / F
10. Sean lives on a farm. T / F
11. Sean doesn't get pocket money. T / F
12. His favourite food is pizza and hamburgers. T / F

▶ SB p. 10

6 Complete the timetable.

	Monday	Tuesday	Wednesday	Thursday	Friday
9-9.55 a.m.	I.T.	Biology	Science	Science	English
10-10.55	English	English	History	French	French
BREAK					
11.15 a.m.-12.10 p.m.	English	Maths	English	English	History
LUNCH					
1-1.55 p.m.	Art	Music	I.T.	Maths	Biology
2-2.35	Art	Science		Music	P.E.
2.40-3.15	Maths	French		Biology	P.E.

7 Who has got what on Monday at 1 o'clock? Write sentences.

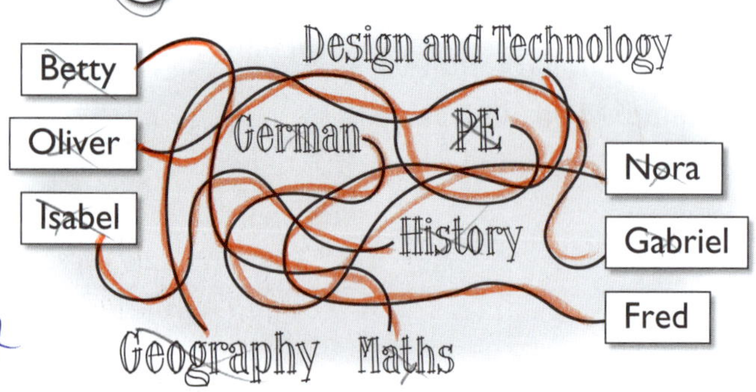

Example: *Betty's got Maths on Monday at 1 o'clock.*

1 Oliver's got P.E. on Monday at 1 o'clock
2 Isabel's got History on Monday at 1 o'clock
3 Nora's got German on Monday at 1 o'clock
4 Gabriel's got Geography on Monday at 1 o'clock
5 Fred's got Design and Technology on Monday at 1 o'clock

8 Match the sentence halves about the blue ring octopus.

1 On the first day of the new school
2 Sara's story was the first
3 Sara and her family went
4 They had a great time swimming and
5 One day Sara's brother came
6 There was a strange blue and
7 Sara remembered about the blue ring
8 She saved her brother's life because

[7] octopus and hit her brother's hand.
[5] back from the beach with a beautiful shell.
[8] the octopus can kill you with one bite.
[1] year the kids told their holiday stories.
[4] playing on the beach.
[2] and also the only story.
[3] to Australia.
[6] yellow thing inside and he wanted to pull it out.

SB p. 10

Grammar Present simple (questions)

■ **9** **Complete the questions.**

Interviewer Where does the blue ring octopus live?

Expert It lives in warm water.

Interviewer 1 How many arms does he have?

Expert It's got eight arms.

Interviewer 2 What colours does it have?

Expert It's dark yellow but it can turn bright yellow. And it has blue rings, of course.

Interviewer 3 What ....?

Expert It eats fish.

Interviewer 4 Is ....?

Expert Yes, the poison is very strong. It can kill a man.

Interviewer 5 Is ....?

Expert No, there's no medicine against the poison. So it's very dangerous.

Grammar Past simple

■ **10** **Find the twelve past forms (→←↑↓↘↗).**

fell ....

....

....

....

....

....

U	W	Z	D	K	T
M	C	R	A	L	O
S	A	F	E	L	L
A	M	W	R	H	D
W	E	R	E	N	A
U	A	A	A	N	H
L	R	B	H	I	T
D	I	A	S	E	Q

● **11** **Match the pictures with the sentences.**

1 In the morning I watched TV.
2 At lunchtime I played computer games.
3 In the afternoon I played beach volleyball.
4 In the evening I went to the cinema.
5 And after the cinema I read a book.
6 After my holidays I was really tired.

▶ SB p. 12

■ **12** **Find the verbs in the word snake and write them in the past simple.**

sitholdremembermeetgoloveread takerunput

1 sit — sat 5 .... — .... 8 .... — ....
2 .... — .... 6 .... — .... 9 .... — ....
3 .... — .... 7 .... — .... 10 .... — ....
4 .... — ....

★ **13** **Write the verbs in brackets* in the past simple.**

The shell on the beach

I [1] saw (see) a really nice shell on the beach. I [2] picked (pick) it up because I [3] wanted (want) to show it to mum. "Oh Michael," mum [4] said (say), "that looks lovely. What a nice shell." "And it's got something blue and yellow inside. Do you want to see it?" I said.

Suddenly my sister Sara [5] hit (hit) my hand and [6] shouted (shout): "Don't touch it." "Ouch!" I [7] said (say). "What's wrong?" "Sara!" mum [8] said (say), "leave Michael alone." "But look!" Sara [9] shouted (shout), and [10] pointed (point) at the nice shell. "There's a blue ring octopus inside. It can kill you!"

There in the sand, there [11] was (be) a little octopus. It [12] looked (look) nice, but mum [13] said (say), "Don't touch it!" And she [14] hugged (hug) me and then she [15] hugged (hug) Sara.

Vocabulary: * bracket – Klammer

★ **14** **Write sentences about Olivia's holiday last month.**

go

Example:
Olivia went to a museum.

see

1 ....

go

2 ....

swim

3 ....

play

4 ....

talk

5 ....

enjoy

6 ....

▶ SB p. 13

Word File

My timetable

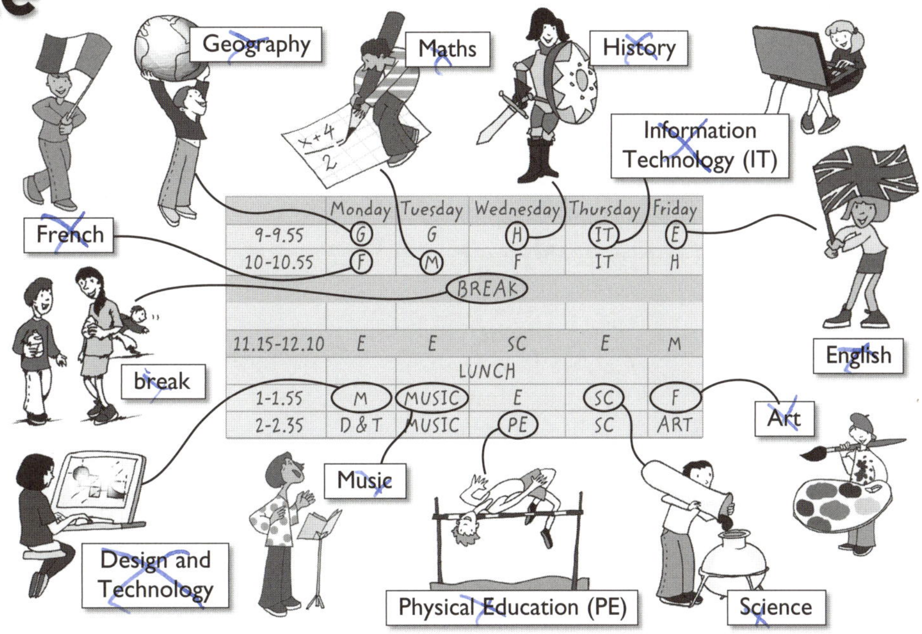

MORE Words and Phrases

2	**mile**	*I live ten miles from here.*	Meile
	type	*What type of holiday do you like?*	Art; Typ; Sorte
	action	*There's an action film on TV tonight.*	Handlung; Aktion
	pocket money	*Everyone gets more pocket money than me!*	Taschengeld
	jewellery	*She spends lots of money on jewellery.*	Schmuck
7	other	*We didn't hear any other stories.*	andere, r, s
	somewhere	*They always go somewhere exciting.*	irgendwo
	everyone	*Come here, everyone!*	jede/r; alle
	air	*How does a plane stay up in the air?*	Luft
	north	*My uncle lives in the north of England.*	nördlich, Nord-; Norden
	on one's own	*Joe wasn't married. He lived on his own.*	allein, auf sich gestellt
	shell	*I like collecting shells on the beach.*	Muschel
	So what?	*"Sue has got a pony." "So what? My sister has got a horse."*	Na und?
	octopus (pl -es)		Krake
	poisonous	*The blue ring octopus is poisonous.*	giftig
	bite	*This snake's bite is poisonous.*	Biss
9	**against**	*There is no medicine against the poison.*	gegen
	body	*The blue ring octopus has blue rings on its body.*	Körper
	coast	*It lives off the coast of Australia.*	Küste
	size	*What size shoes do you take?*	Größe
	bright	*I love bright colours.*	hell, leuchtend
	hunt	*Some animals hunt at night.*	jagen
	poison		Gift
	attacker	*The insect uses poison to kill its attacker.*	Angreifer/in
	dangerous	*The blue ring octopus is very dangerous.*	gefährlich
	medicine (no pl)	*Do you need medicine?*	Medizin, Medikament(e)
12	shake	*Did you shake the octopus' arm?*	schütteln
	sight	*This is quite a sight!*	Aussicht, Anblick
13	furious	*She's got ink on her new jeans – she's furious.*	wütend
	ink		Tinte
	cover	*Cover the computer before ink gets on that, too!*	bedecken
	back	*I hurt my back when I fell over.*	Rücken
	hug	*We hugged each other and said goodbye.*	umarmen
	tight	*My shoes are too tight.*	fest; eng

UNIT 2 Did we catch them?

Revision

● 1 **What's the subject? Write the subject underneath the picture.**

1 ...French... 2 ...Music... 3 .... 4 ....

5 .... 6 .... 7 .... 8 ....

■ 2 **Write the verb in brackets in the past simple.** **Vocabulary:** *spot – Fleck, dunkle Stelle

Yesterday my friends and I [1] ...went... (go) to the beach. We [2] ...played... (play) some beach volleyball and then we [3] ...sat... (sit) down on the sand. Suddenly my friend Sheryl [4] ...shouted... (shout) and [5] ...pointed... (point) at the sand. There were lots and lots of little spiders. Two or three were on our legs, and some were on our clothes. "Are they poisonous?" Sheryl [6] ...asked... (ask). "Not really," I said, "but when they bite you it hurts and you get a red spot.* Let's go to another place." We [7] ...got... (get) up, [8] ...put... (put) our clothes somewhere else and [9] ...went... (go) for a long swim.

★ 3 **Complete with the verbs in the box in the past simple.**

~~stay~~
~~watch~~
~~go~~
~~are~~
~~is~~
~~get up~~
~~read~~
~~go~~

I [1] ...went... to France with my parents last summer. We [2] ...stayed... in a little village in Burgundy. Every morning my dad [3] ...got up... early and [4] ...went... for a long walk. My mum and I [5] ...watched... a bit of TV ('It helps my French,' my mum said), and then we had lunch. In the afternoons we went shopping, or went for a drive in the country. There [6] ...was... a small swimming pool in the garden of our house. That was nice. But for me, the holidays [7] ...were... a bit boring. I don't like shopping. But I had a lot of time for reading. I [8] ...read... all the Harry Potter books again.

END OF REVISION SECTION

4 **Find the words and write them under the pictures. (↓ →)**

1 ....

2 ....

A	S	S	I	S	T	A	N	T
S	W	T	C	H	E	M	F	E
S	A	G	J	E	W	E	L	S
I	T	E	E	T	A	D	O	T
T	C	O	L	H	L	A	O	O
A	H	S	W	A	L	L	R	I
C	S	T	A	G	E	W	B	F
H	Y	P	N	O	T	I	S	T

8 ....

7 ....

3 ....

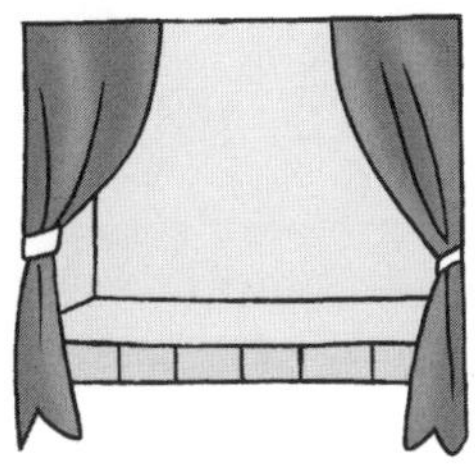

4 ....

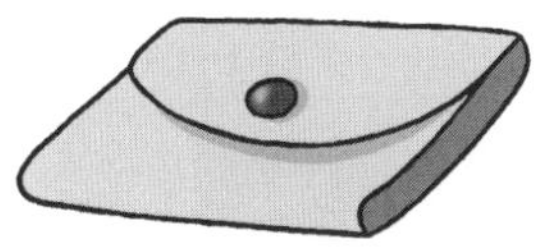

5 ....

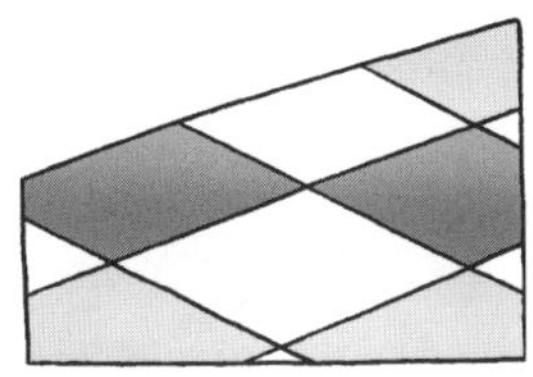

6 ....

5 **Read about the play *Pronto*! Underline the six mistakes.**

Roger and Claire went to a hypnotist show. The hypnotist, Charles, hypnotised Roger with a watch. The hypnotist took Roger's wallet from him. Roger woke up when the hypnotist said 'Abracadabra'.

But the man also gave Roger some secret commands. Roger broke into a shop and stole some jewels. Then he jumped out of the window.

But he left his wallet there, and the police found it. Inspector Lime went to Roger and Claire's house to investigate* the crime. But Roger wasn't there – he was in hospital.

Sergeant Lewis went to the hospital with Claire to talk to Roger, but he didn't react. Roger woke up when a doctor said the secret word. Claire told the police about the hypnotist.

The police caught the hypnotist and his friend in Hong Kong.

Vocabulary: *investigate – untersuchen

6 **Write sentences. Correct the mistakes in 5.**

1 *Charles hypnotised Roger with a medal.*

2 ....

3 ....

4 ....

5 ....

6 ....

▶ SB p. 18

● 7 Complete the dialogue with the words in the box.

find found ~~took~~ take have use put jumped

A Did you hear about the robbery last week?

B No. What happened?

A Two men broke into a bank in the High Street. They [1]......took...... a lot of money and [2].............................. it into bags. Then they [3].................................. out of a window.

B Why didn't they [4]................................ the door?

A They didn't [5]... the key!

B Oh, right! Did the police find them?

A No – but they [6].................................. the money!

B Really? Where did they [7]...................................... it?

A In the bank. The two men didn't [8]... the bags with them!!

■ 8 Put the dialogue in the correct order.

☐ **Lewis** Did they talk to you?

☐ **Lewis** Why did he hit him?

☐ **Lewis** Did you and your friends go to the bank?

☐ **Lewis** Did you see anyone in the bar?

1 **Lewis** Where were you at 8 o'clock last night?

☐ **Man** No, we didn't. We went to a bar.

☐ **Man** Yes, I did. I saw two men. They were at another table.

☐ **Man** No, they didn't. But one man looked very angry and he hit the other man!

☐ **Man** I was in High Street. I went there with my friends.

☐ **Man** I don't know – but he shouted 'You fool! Why did you leave the bags in the bank?'

★ 9 Do the puzzle. Write the past simple of the verbs and find the secret word.

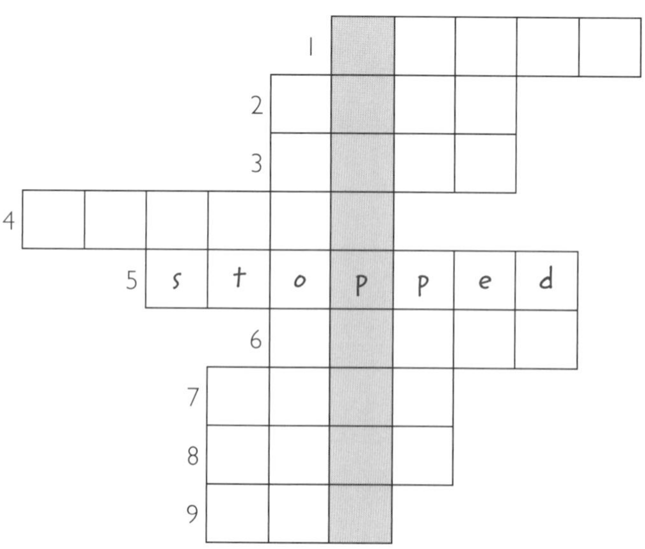

1 find
2 take
3 tell
4 catch
5 ~~stop~~
6 break
7 say
8 go
9 get

The secret word is ....

▶ SB p. 18

★ **10** **Look at the pictures. Continue the story.**
Use the words in the box below to help you.

The missing money

broke the vase	angry
found the money	picked up
fell over the cat	gave
went to her house	jumped
very happy	~~phoned~~
saw a vase	

One day Mrs Jones phoned Inspector Lime. She said: 'I can't find my money.' Inspector Lime went . . . .

....

....

....

....

Grammar Past simple (negative)

■ **11** **Complete with the words in the box.**

~~went~~
didn't go
didn't have
found
didn't find
had
took
didn't take

Bill Gunn and Tony Bull stole money from the bank last night. They [1] ....went.... to the bank and broke a window. They [2] .... the money from the safe and put it in bags. Then they jumped out of a window. They [3] .... out through* the door because they [4] .... the key. But Bill [5] .... the bags with him! The police [6] .... the thieves, but they [7] .... the money. Bill and Tony [8] .... a big argument* in a bar – they were really angry!

Vocabulary: *through – durch / argument – Streit

▶ SB p. **18**

■ **12** **Write the verbs in brackets in the past simple.**

Hi Simone,

I [1] ......didn't phone...... (not phone) you, because the phone [2] .... (not work). And I [3] .... (not send) you an email, because the computer [4] .... (not work). And I [5] .... (not buy) you a present, because I [6] .... (not have) any money. And I [7] .... (not get) you any chocolate, because I [8] .... (not know) which chocolate you like. So I [9] .... (not go) to your party and I [10] .... (not make) a birthday cake for you. But happy birthday anyway!

Grammar Past simple (questions and short answers)

★ **13** **Complete the questions and the short answers.**

1 **A** ......Did...... they ......arrive...... after midnight? (arrive)
B Yes, ...they did...... .

2 **A** .... you .... your trip? (enjoy)
B No, ...

3 **A** .... your parents .... with you? (go)
B No, ...

4 **A** .... you .... a lot? (swim)
B Yes, ...

5 **A** .... you .... by bus? (go)
B Yes, ...

6 **A** .... she .... you a postcard? (write)
B No, ...

7 **A** .... they .... the hotel? (like)
B No, ...

8 **A** .... your mum .... a lot? (talk)
B No, she ....

★ **14** **Answer the questions for you.**

1 Did you go to school yesterday?
....

2 Did you phone any friends yesterday?
....

3 Did your best friend phone you yesterday?
....

4 Did you watch TV last night?
....

5 Did you go to the cinema last weekend?
....

6 Did your class have a test last week?
....

▶ SB p. 19

Word File Police

MORE Words and Phrases

1	stage		Bühne
	wallet	*I have my money in my wallet.*	Brieftasche
	floor	*The wallet is on the floor.*	Boden
2	**address**	*What's your address?*	Adresse
	already	*I've already seen it.*	bereits, schon
	both	*They both laugh.*	beide
	I don't care.		Es macht mir nichts aus.
	important	*Please talk to me, it's very important.*	wichtig
	office	*Inspector Lime's office is at the police station.*	Büro
	plane	*They were on a plane to Singapore.*	Flugzeug
	still	*It was late, but the streets were still full of people.*	noch, noch immer
	play		Spiel; Theaterstück
	character	*What character are you in the play?*	Charakter; hier: Person
	girlfriend	*Roger's new girlfriend is very clever.*	Freundin
	doctor	*I'm ill! I need a doctor.*	Arzt/Ärztin
	scene	*In the last scene of the play I fell asleep.*	Szene
	gentleman		Gentleman; Herr
	applause	*The applause at the end of the play was very loud.*	Beifall
	seat	*This theatre has 1,000 seats.*	(Sitz)platz
	swing	*The hypnotist was swinging a watch in front of me.*	(hin- und her)schwingen
	command	*The boss gives commands.*	Befehl
	do the washing-up	*Do the washing-up – and do it pronto!*	abwaschen
	kiss	*My mum kissed me and said goodnight.*	küssen
	work	*My dad works in the bank.*	arbeiten; funktionieren
	secret	*Sssh! I'll tell you a secret.*	Geheimnis; geheim
	jewel		Juwel
	clean	*My shoes are clean.*	sauber
	dirty	*I must clean my dirty shoes.*	dreckig, schmutzig
	react	*Ms Black did not react.*	reagieren
	stiff	*My neck's stiff. I can't move my head.*	steif
	solve	*Inspector Todd solved the mystery.*	lösen
	fact	*Tell me the facts.*	Fakten, Tatsachen
3	**belong**	*That doesn't belong to me.*	gehören
	worth	*It was worth it.*	wert sein
6	**large**	*I saw a man with a large bag.*	groß

UNIT 3 Oops!

Revision

● 1 **Complete the text with the words in the box.**

jumped
fell
took
pick
find
phoned

1 **A** What did he do with the bags?
B He [1] .... them with him.

2 **A** Can you buy the tickets?
B Sorry, I can't [2] .... my wallet.

3 **A** What's wrong?
B My leg hurts. I just [3] .... over the cat.

4 **A** How did you catch the thief?
B I [4] .... the police.

5 **A** Where's the cat?
B I think it [5] .... up that tree.

6 **A** Where are the bags?
B Sorry, I forgot to [6] .... them up.

■ 2 **Complete with the words in the box in the past simple.**

~~not~~ find
~~not take~~
not eat
~~not~~ sit
~~not have~~
~~not~~ go

Last weekend we went to Paris. We [1] ...didn't take... the ferry*, because mum doesn't like boats. We went by train*, but we [2] ...didn't sit... down because the train was very full. In Paris we [3] ...didn't find... our hotel at the beginning. When we found it, they [4] ...didn't have... three rooms so I was in a room with my uncle. We walked to the Eiffel Tower, but we [5] ...didn't go... up because there were thousands of tourists. Then we went to a restaurant, but we [6] ...did not eat... very nice food. The next day was better – we went to the country and spent the day there.

Vocabulary: * ferry – Fähre / train – Zug

■ 3 **Complete the questions.**

Inspector Fry [1] .... (see / bank robber)?
Girl Yes, I did.
Inspector Fry What [2] .... (look like)?
Girl Well, he looked like a bank robber.
Inspector Fry What [3] .... (mean)?
Girl Well, he had a gun and a large bag.
Inspector Fry What [4] .... you .... (do) when you saw him?
Girl Nothing.
Inspector Fry Why [5] .... you .... (not run) after him?
Girl Inspector, isn't that your job?

END OF REVISION SECTION

● **4** **Put the sentences in the correct order to tell the stories about Mr Custer and Caroline Smith.**

The cup-holder

- [ ] After two weeks he phoned the computer shop because he had a problem.
- [ ] "The one with the cup-holder," Mr Custer said.
- [1] Mr Custer bought a really good computer with a DVD and a flat screen.
- [ ] "A computer with a cup-holder?" – The shop assistant didn't understand.
- [ ] The cup-holder was, in fact, the DVD-drive.
- [ ] "What kind of computer have you got?" the shop assistant asked him.

Modern art

- [ ] One day the director told her to clean a room on the first floor.
- [1] Caroline Smith was a cleaning lady in a Museum of Modern Art.
- [ ] The windows were clean but part of a modern sculpture was missing.
- [ ] "Those old roses?" she answered. "I threw them away."
- [ ] "Where are the roses from the sculpture?" asked the director.
- [ ] Two hours later the director went upstairs to check on her work.

● **5** **Read this text of the story on page 22 in the Student's Book. There is one mistake in each sentence. Underline the mistake and write the correct word(s).**

The wrong uncle

1 Mrs Browning and her <u>son</u> were at Gatwick airport in London.
........husband........

2 They wanted to pick up Mrs Browning's uncle who was on a plane from Boston.
....

3 It was the second meeting between Mrs Browning and her uncle.
....

4 Mrs Browning had a photo of him in her pocket.
....

5 Mrs Browning saw her uncle. He had a black coat on.
....

6 Mrs Browning ran over to the man and said hello.
....

7 They took him to the bus station.
....

8 They put the man on the bus but he tried to jump out.
....

9 "Take my passport," he said. "Please let me go!"
....

10 The man was not Mrs Browning's uncle, but a stranger flying to Rome.
....

▶ SB p. 22

6 Make sentences about the stories on page 22 in the Student's Book.

~~Mr Custer~~	thought	~~a new computer.~~
Caroline Smith	worked	a room with a sculpture in it.
Mrs Browning	went	a work of art*.
	~~bought~~	his DVD-drive was a cup-holder.
	threw away	to her uncle and kissed him.
	ran over	in an art museum.
	phoned	her uncle into the car.
	pushed	to Gatwick airport.
	cleaned	the computer shop.

Mr Custer bought a new computer.

....

....

....

....

....

....

....

Vocabulary: * work of art – Kunstwerk

7 Write in the correct word.

luggage*
nights
passport*
sleep
sweater
taxi
~~tickets~~
window

Leonie Charles, have you got the plane [1] *tickets* ?
Charles Of course I've got them.
Leonie And have you got your [2] .... ?
Charles Of course I've got it. Have you got your passport?
Leonie Yes. Did you call a [3] .... ?
Charles Of course, I did. It's going to pick us up in ten minutes.
Leonie And did you pack your warm [4] .... ?
Charles No, Leonie, I didn't. We're going to Sicily. It's hot there.
Leonie Maybe the [5] .... are cold.
Charles Maybe. But I'm not going to [6] .... in my sweater.
Leonie OK. Let's go, the taxi's waiting.

(An hour later at the airport.)

Leonie Charles, can you check in our [7] .... ?
Charles Of course.
Leonie And Charles? I want a [8] .... seat.
Charles Sure. There's only one problem, Leonie.
Leonie What is it?
Charles I'm looking at our tickets.
Leonie And?
Charles And – our flight is tomorrow!

Vocabulary:
* passport – Reisepass
luggage – Gepäck

▶ SB p. 23

● **8** **Read the dialogue on page 18 again. Circle T (*True*) or F (*False*).**

1 Charles can't find the tickets. **T / F**
2 Charles has got his passport. **T / F**
3 Leonie can't find her passport. **T / F**
4 Charles called a taxi. **T / F**
5 They are going to Sicily. **T / F**
6 It's very cold there. **T / F**
7 Leonie wants a window seat. **T / F**
8 They leave one hour late. **T / F**

Grammar *because*

★ **9** **Look at the pictures and write sentences with *because*. Use the words in the box.**

~~phone him~~
go to the dentist's*
have toothache*
see a face at the window
have a cold*
stay in bed
~~be happy~~
be scared

Vocabulary:
*dentist – Zahnarzt/-ärztin
toothache – Zahnschmerzen
cold – Erkältung

1 *He was happy because Janice phoned him.*

2 ....

3 ....

4 ....

● **10** **Match the questions and answers.**

1 Why are you late?
2 Why did you tell her? It was a secret.
3 Why did you get a cat?
4 Why is he so happy?
5 Why did you buy a new computer?
6 Why are you taking a sweater?
7 Why is he so angry?
8 Why did the police visit him?

☐ Because I don't like dogs.
☐ Because I missed my bus.
☐ Because his football team didn't win.
☐ Because my old one hasn't got a DVD-drive.
☐ Because he got an 'A' in the test.
☐ Because she's my friend.
☐ Because they think he's a thief.
☐ Because it's going to be cold tonight.

▶ SB p. 24

★ **11 Use your own ideas to write answers to these questions.**

1 Why did you buy me this present?
Because I wanted to make you happy.

2 Why did you turn off the TV?
....

3 Why didn't you go to school?
....

4 Why didn't you eat breakfast?
....

5 Why are you so tired today?
....

6 Why haven't you got any money?
....

Grammar *one/ones*

● **12 Complete the sentences with *one* or *ones*.**

1 **A** Which bike is yours?
B The green ....

2 **A** Do you like my jeans?
B They're not bad, but I like the grey .... better.

3 **A** Did you see the photo?
B Yes, I saw the .... you took on Sunday.

4 **A** My computer doesn't work very well!
B Why don't you buy a new ....

5 **A** Which are your favourite glasses?
B The blue ....

6 **A** Which picture do you like?
B The .... of the dog.

■ **13 Write mini-dialogues for the pictures. Use the example to help you.**

A *I'd like to try some glasses on.*
B *Which ones — the red ones or the blue ones?*
A *The red ones.*

A ....
B ....
A ....

A ....
B ....
A ....

A ....
B ....
A ....

▶ SB p. 25

MORE Words and Phrases

1	**airport**	*They wanted to pick him up from the airport.*	Flughafen
	between	*It was the first meeting between Mrs Browning and her uncle.*	zwischen
	meeting		Treffen, Begegnung
	in fact	*It's hot today, in fact it's very hot!*	genau genommen
	push	*He pushed the man into the car.*	schieben, drücken
	which	*Which man is your uncle?*	welche, r, s
	drive	*'First, put the DVD in the DVD-drive.'*	Laufwerk
	upstairs	*The modern art is upstairs.*	(nach) oben
	screen	*I have a picture of my cat on my computer screen.*	Leinwand; Bildschirm
	uncle	*My uncle and aunt live in America.*	Onkel
	coat	*Please leave your coat here.*	Mantel
	car park	*The car park is free at weekends.*	Parkplatz
	flight	*This is a non-smoking flight.*	Flug
	complete	*He's a complete stranger.*	vollständig
	stranger	*Do you know him – or is he a stranger?*	Fremde/r
2	**part**	*Part of the modern sculpture was missing.*	Teil
	work	*Will you help me with my work?*	Arbeit
3	fireman	*The fireman told the fire chief about the accident.*	Feuerwehrmann
	fire brigade	*Call the fire brigade! The house is on fire!*	Feuerwehr
4	what's wrong	*Why? What's wrong with the blue one?*	Was ist los?; Stimmt etwas nicht?
5	**explain**	*I don't understand – please explain.*	erklären
	teapot	*I broke the teapot and all the cups.*	Teekanne
6	**could**	*It's something you could do.*	könnte, könntest, könnten, könntet
7	**funny**	*It's not funny.*	lustig, komisch
8	**paint**	*I want to paint my bedroom red.*	malen, (an)streichen
	sleep	*I was tired because I didn't sleep much.*	schlafen

UNIT 4 Halloween

Revision

● **1 Do the puzzle and find the secret word.**

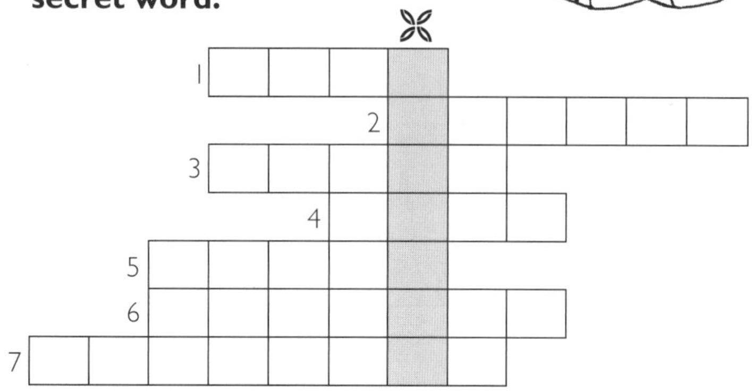

The secret word is ....

■ **2 Match the questions and answers.**

1	Why are you sad?	☐	Because he stole the money.
2	Why didn't you phone me?	☐	Because their old one didn't work any more.
3	Why did the detective arrest Mr Brown?	1	Because my cat ran away a week ago.
4	Why didn't Annie go to the cinema?	☐	Because she didn't have any money.
5	Why did they buy a new car?	☐	Because I didn't have my phone with me.

● **3 Complete with *one* or *ones*.**

Vocabulary: *plate – Teller

END OF REVISION SECTION

■ 4 Do the crossword*.

Across*:

1 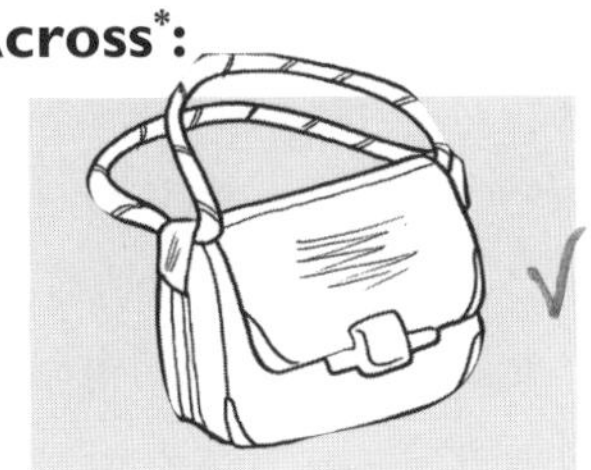 √

5 It shines in the night. √

6 A house with a ghost in it is … . √

9  √

■	■	1 B	A	2 G	■	3 F
■	4 S	■	■	H	■	U
■	W	■	5 M	O	O	N
■	E	■	■	S	■	■
6 H	A	U	N	T	E	7 D
■	T	■	■	■	■	O
■	■	8 A	■	■	■	W
9 P	U	M	P	K	I	N

Down:

2  √

3 At Halloween kids want to have … .

4 At Halloween the kids ask for a … √

7 The opposite* of up √

8 A form of *be* √

Vocabulary: *crossword – Kreuzworträtsel
across – waagrecht / opposite – Gegenteil

● 5 Write the words under the pictures.

a haunted castle
a candle
knock on a door
a vampire
a witch
cut off the top
a scary face
a pumpkin

a 
a witch

b 
pumpkin

c 
a vampire

d 
a haunted castle

e 
knsch on the door

f 
a scary face

g 
a candle

h 
cut off the top

▶ SB p. 27

■ 6 Match the sentence halves of the story *Trick or treat.*

1 Last Halloween Larry and Kerry went to
2 There they met a
3 Together they went to an old house. It
4 An old man opened the door and
5 Jim wanted to play a trick
6 Suddenly the door opened, then it closed
7 Larry and Kerry went home and
8 The chief inspector told

[5] on the old man. He put superglue into the lock.
[7] told their parents and the police.
[6] again and Jim wasn't there anymore.
[1] play 'trick or treat' on the other side of the town.
[9] them: "The house has been empty for 20 years."
[2] boy. His name was Jim.
[4] said: "Go away."
[3] looked like a house from a horror film.

● 7 *Halloween* – 20 years later – read the text and put the pictures into the correct order.

1 Twenty years later my brother Larry and I went to the house again. "Let's knock at the door," Larry said to me.
2 We went up to the house, but I was a bit scared.
3 Larry laughed at me and knocked. Nothing happened. We started to walk away.
4 Then a man came out of the house. He looked like Jim but twenty years older.
5 "At last you are here," he said. "Come in, come in." And he took my brother by the hand.
6 I shouted and pulled Larry away. Then we ran.
7 We heard a very loud sigh* coming from the house.
8 Then the house collapsed*.

Vocabulary:
*sigh – Seufzer
collapsed – stürzte ein

▶ SB p. 28

■ **8** **Complete the dialogue with the sentences in the box. There are three sentences that you do not need.**

~~And don't stay out very~~ late.
~~Can we go now, Mum~~?
Have we got another black hat?
~~Thanks~~, Mum.
That's a lot of chocolate.
Trick or treat, Aunt* Melinda.
~~Yes, I've got it, Mum. Can~~ we go ~~now~~?

Vocabulary: *aunt – Tante

Mum Let me look at you. Oh, great! You look nice and scary!
Allie Thanks, Mum. 1 Can we go now, Mum?
Mum Yes, but be careful. Always stay with Jimmy.
Allie I know, Mum.
Jimmy Yeah, Mum, we know. Don't worry.
Mum 2 And don't stay out very late
Jimmy Until ten. Is that OK?
Mum OK. And have you got your mobile?
Allie 3 Yes, I've got it, Mum. Can we go now?
Mum Yes, of course. Have fun.
Jimmy 4 Thanks Mum
Allie Bye Mum!
Mum And Jimmy? Have you got the bag for the sweets?
Jimmy Oh, Mum!

★ **9** **Write the story behind the pictures.**

One Halloween, two children knocked on the door …
An old woman* … .
She looked like …
The children said: " …
The old woman said: " …
She went back …
After some minutes she …
Behind her were …
They laughed and shouted …
The children …

One Halloween, two children knocked on the door and waited till someone opened it. An old woman opened it. She looked like a witch! The children screamed: "Run!" When they started to run she said: "Wait!" The two children slowly went back and saw, behind her were women that had on costumes. They laughed and shouted. The children then got some sweets.

Vocabulary: *woman – Frau

▶ SB p. **29**

Grammar *should/shouldn't*

Vocabulary: *vet – Tierarzt/-ärztin

■ **10 Match the dialogues.**

1 I'm scared at Halloween.
2 I'm tired.
3 I'm hungry.
4 My head hurts.
5 My mum's angry with me.
6 My cat's ill.
7 It's raining outside.
8 It's a very scary film.

[2] You shouldn't go to bed so late.
[4] You should take an aspirin.
[5] You should say you're sorry.
[6] You should take it to the vet*.
[7] You should take an umbrella.
[1] You shouldn't leave the house then.
[8] You shouldn't watch it alone.
[3] You should eat an apple.

● **11 Write the sentences under the pictures.**

~~She~~ should see a doctor.
~~He should~~ go to bed.
~~He shouldn't~~ eat so much.
~~He~~ should invite her to ~~the cinema~~.
~~He shouldn't~~ drive so fast.
~~He~~ shouldn't go in there.

1 He should go to bed

2 He shouldn't eat so much

3 He should invite her to the cinema

4 He shouldn't drive so fast

5 She should see a doctor

6 He shouldn't go in there

■ **12 Here is what parents say to their kids at Halloween. Write *should* or *shouldn't*.**

1 You should say thank you when you get a treat.
2 You shouldn't scare very small kids.
3 You shouldn't go into houses of people you don't know.
4 You shouldn't eat too many sweets.
5 You should take your mobile with you.
6 You shouldn't stay out too long.

▶ SB p. 31

Word File

Halloween

In a haunted castle

MORE Words and Phrases

2	windy	*It's often windy in November.*	windig
	be lost	*Our dog is lost again. He always runs off.*	sich verirrt haben
3	**tradition**	*Trick or treating is a tradition at Halloween.*	Tradition
	aged (11)		(11) Jahre alt
	etc. (et cetera)	*We brought the cups, glasses, etc.*	usw., etc.
4	far away	*My house is far away from here.*	weit weg
	other side	*It's on the other side of town.*	andere Seite
	should	*We should go in there.*	sollten, sollen
5	twin	*These two boys are twins.*	Zwilling, Zwillings-
	age	*They are the same age.*	Alter
	(door) **lock**	*I turned the key in the lock and opened the door.*	(Tür)Schloss
	disappear	*Come back soon – don't disappear!*	verschwinden
8	**shut**	*He shut the door quickly.*	schließen, zumachen
11	**most**	*Ghosts scare me most.*	am meisten, die meisten
12	**keen (on)**	*I'm not so keen on maths.*	begeistert (über)
	kick	*Ouch! That was a hard kick!*	Tritt, Stoß

Revision

● 1 **Write the words in the correct places.**

Vocabulary: *fingernail – Fingernagel

moon
pumpkin
witch
ghost
vampire
fingernails*
midnight
candle

■ 2 **Match the sentences.**

1 My head hurts.
2 I'm bored!
3 I got my test back. It's terrible.
4 I'm very, very tired.
5 I'm sorry, I'm late again!
6 There's a ghost in our house!

☐ You should work harder.
☐ You should leave the house earlier.
[1] You should take an aspirin.
☐ You should call a ghost hunter.
☐ You should read a book.
☐ You should go to bed.

END OF REVISION SECTION

3 Complete this story. Write *Bacon, Judith* or *Jeff*.

Judith Crowe, her son Jeff and his pet pig Bacon went swimming in the river on a hot day. 1 .... was only five years old and his pet pig was better at swimming than him.

They played and swam for an hour. Then 2 .... got out of the water. 3 .... swam into the middle of the river, where the water was deeper and more dangerous. He was in trouble.

4 .... jumped into the water and tried to swim to her son. But 5 .... was faster than her and got to the boy first.

6 .... put his arms round the pig. But he was bigger and heavier than 7 .... They went under the water. But suddenly 8 .... saw 9 .... come out of the water on 10 ....'s back!! She was very happy.

Grammar Comparatives

4 Complete with the comparative form of the adjectives.

1 **A** The pizza at Tony's is ....better.... (good) than the pizza at Little Italy.
B You're right.

2 **A** It's very hot today.
B Yes, but it was much ....hotter.... (hot) yesterday.

3 **A** My bag is ....heavier.... (heavy) than yours.
B Well, I'm not carrying so many books around.

4 **A** A Ferrari is ....faster.... (fast) than a Porsche.
B True, and it's ....more expensive.... (expensive*) than a Porsche.

5 **A** How much ....older.... (old) than you is your brother?
B Three years. He was fifteen in June.

6 **A** I really like our new gym*. It's much ....bigger.... (big) than the old one.
B That's true, but the old one was ....better.... (good).

Vocabulary: *expensive – teuer / gym (gymnasium) – Turnsaal/Turnhalle

5 Write the adjectives under the pictures.

strong
heavy
friendly
big
small
dangerous
hairy
clever

1 ....

2 ....

3 ....

4 ....

5 ....

6 ....

7 ....

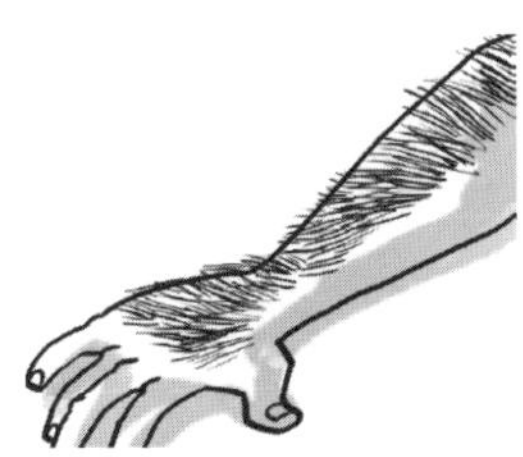
8 ....

▶ SB p. 32

★ **6** **Read the text and circle T (*True*) or F (*False*).**

Ricky's safari trip

Last year we went on safari to Africa. It was great – we saw lots of brilliant birds and animals. I really liked the rhino that we saw one day – it was very big (about 1.5m high) and I'm sure it was really heavy, too. The guide* said that sometimes a rhino can weigh 2,000 kilograms! But I wasn't scared. My father told me that rhinos aren't very dangerous animals. Rhinos are almost blind and so they can't see well. There were lots of small grey and white birds on the rhinoceros' back. I think the birds eat very small insects from the rhino's skin.

Later the same day we saw some baboons*. There was a big family of them. I thought they looked nice and friendly, but we didn't go very close. You have to be careful, because male* baboons are strong and they aren't very friendly! Some people think baboons are very intelligent too. I don't know about that, but I'm sure they're more intelligent than rhinos!

At the end of the day, when we went back to the hotel – guess what? In my parents' room there was a big, black, hairy tarantula*! My father was really scared, but my mother just picked it up and put it outside. My mum's really cool!

1	Ricky liked the rhino.	T / F
2	Rhinos are very dangerous animals.	T / F
3	Rhinos can't see very well.	T / F
4	They went very close to the baboons.	T / F
5	Male baboons are strong and friendly.	T / F
6	Ricky is sure that rhinos are not as intelligent as baboons.	T / F
7	The tarantula was in Ricky's bedroom at the hotel.	T / F
8	Ricky's mother put the tarantula outside.	T / F

Vocabulary:

*guide – Führer
skin – Haut
baboon – Pavian
male – männlich
tarantula – Tarantel

★ **7** **Put the text in the correct order.**

- ☐ a lot. Their favourite pet was the Ruckle – it was half
- ☐ as the Hipcop. There were other animals that the Atlantians
- 1 The people who lived in Atlantis liked animals
- ☐ land animal and half bird, but it didn't fly. The Ruckle
- ☐ didn't keep as pets. One of them was a small
- ☐ very beautiful, but it wasn't as ugly as the Snapkle.
- ☐ dangerous – as dangerous as a blue ring octopus. It wasn't
- ☐ reptile called the Bugboy. The Bugboy was very, very
- ☐ was friendlier than the Hipcop, but it wasn't as clever

▶ SB p. 34

8 **Complete the sentences with the words in the box.**

desert
mosquito
weigh
poisonous
whale
worldwide

1 The Taipan is a very .... snake.
2 The Sahara is a very big .... in Africa.
3 A .... can give you malaria.
4 Some rhinos .... about 2,000 kilos!
5 More than 2 billion people .... speak English.
6 The .... is the biggest mammal in the sea.

Grammar *(not) as ... as*

★ **9** **Read the sentences. Tick the ones you think are true. The answers are on the next page.**

1 The Eiffel Tower isn't as tall as the Empire State Building. ☐
2 The River Nile isn't as long as the River Amazon. ☐
3 There aren't as many people in Switzerland* as in Austria. ☐
4 There aren't as many castles in Finland as in Germany. ☐
5 The blue ring octopus isn't as dangerous as the mosquito. ☐
6 The Estuarine crocodile isn't as long as the Taipan snake. ☐
7 Elephants aren't as heavy as blue whales. ☐
8 Austria isn't as big as Hungary. ☐

Vocabulary:
*Switzerland – die Schweiz

10 **Complete B's answers. Use the same adjective as A.**

1 **A** I don't think squash is exciting. **B** Really? I think it's as exciting as tennis.
2 **A** I don't think rabbits are quiet. **B** Really? I think .... hamsters.
3 **A** I don't think spiders are scary. **B** Really? I think .... snakes.
4 **A** I don't think your dog is clever. **B** Really? I think .... your cat!
5 **A** I don't think this DVD is good. **B** Really? I think .... the other one.
6 **A** I don't think you're very strong. **B** Really? I think .... you!

11 **Complete the text. Use *as ... as* or comparative adjectives.**

A I see you've got all the *Harry Potter* books. What do you think of them?

B I really like all the *Harry Potter* books. I've read them all. I think that *The Chamber of Secrets* is a 1 better (good) book than *The Order of the Phoenix*. *The Chamber of Secrets* is 2 more interesting (interesting) and 3 more exciting (exciting) than *The Order of the Phoenix*. And *The Order of the Phoenix* is much 4 longer (long).

A What do you think of the films?

B Well, *The Philosopher's Stone* film isn't 5 better as (good) the book. I really like the books much 6 better (good) than the films.

A Tell me more about the books.

B Well, *The Goblet of Fire* was 7 better (good) *The Chamber of Secrets*. And *The Chamber of Secrets* was 8 more exciting as (exciting) *The Prisoner of Azkaban*.

A So what should I read?

B Start at the beginning with *The Philosopher's Stone*.

SB p. 34

Grammar Superlatives

★ **12** **Write the words in the correct order to make sentences.**

1 is / Today / yesterday. / colder / than
Today is colder than yesterday.

2 coldest / Yesterday / of the year. / the / was / day
....

3 is / snakes / one of / the / cobra / The / most / in the world. / poisonous
....

4 than / are / Ostriches / people. / faster
....

5 are / Gorillas / chimpanzees. / than / bigger
....

6 longest / Anacondas / the / world. / the / are / snakes / in
....

7 is / best / animals. / book / the / This / about
....

8 the / world? / dangerous / What's / animal / in / most / the
....

★ **13** **Harry, Larry and Barry are brothers – triplets*! Look at the picture and the table and write sentences. Use the adjectives in the box.**

	Harry	Barry	Larry
born*	02/02/90 10.20 a.m.	02/02/90 10.50 a.m.	02/02/90 11.40 a.m.
last school grade*	All 'C's	All 'B's	All 'A's
weight*	70kg	63kg	73kg
running 100m	12.5 seconds	18 seconds	14.6 seconds

~~tall~~
old
heavy
intelligent
short
young
slow
fast

1 *Harry is the tallest.*
2 ....
3 ....
4 ....
5 ....
6 ....
7 ....
8 ....

Vocabulary: *triplets – Drillinge / born – geboren / grade – Note / weight – Gewicht

■ **14** **Answer the questions for you.**

1 Who is the tallest person in your family?
My Dad.

2 What is the best thing in your bedroom?
My bed.

3 What is the heaviest thing in your house or flat?
Our piano is the heaviest.

4 What is the most expensive thing in your house?
One of our paintings.

5 What is the most interesting animal in the world?
Snakes

6 What is your best subject at school?
TEW Technisches Werken

1 True. The Eiffel Tower is 300 metres tall and the Empire State Building is 381 metres tall. 2 Not true. The Nile is longer. 3 True. In Switzerland there are more than 7 million people and in Austria there are a bit more than 8 million. 4 Not true. Finland has more lakes. There are almost 200,000 of them. 5 True. Mosquito bites kill far more people than the bite of the small octopus. 6 Not true. The Estuarine crocodile is much longer. 7 True. The blue whale is the heaviest animal in the world. 8 True. Hungary is bigger than Austria.

▶ SB p. 35

Word File More animals

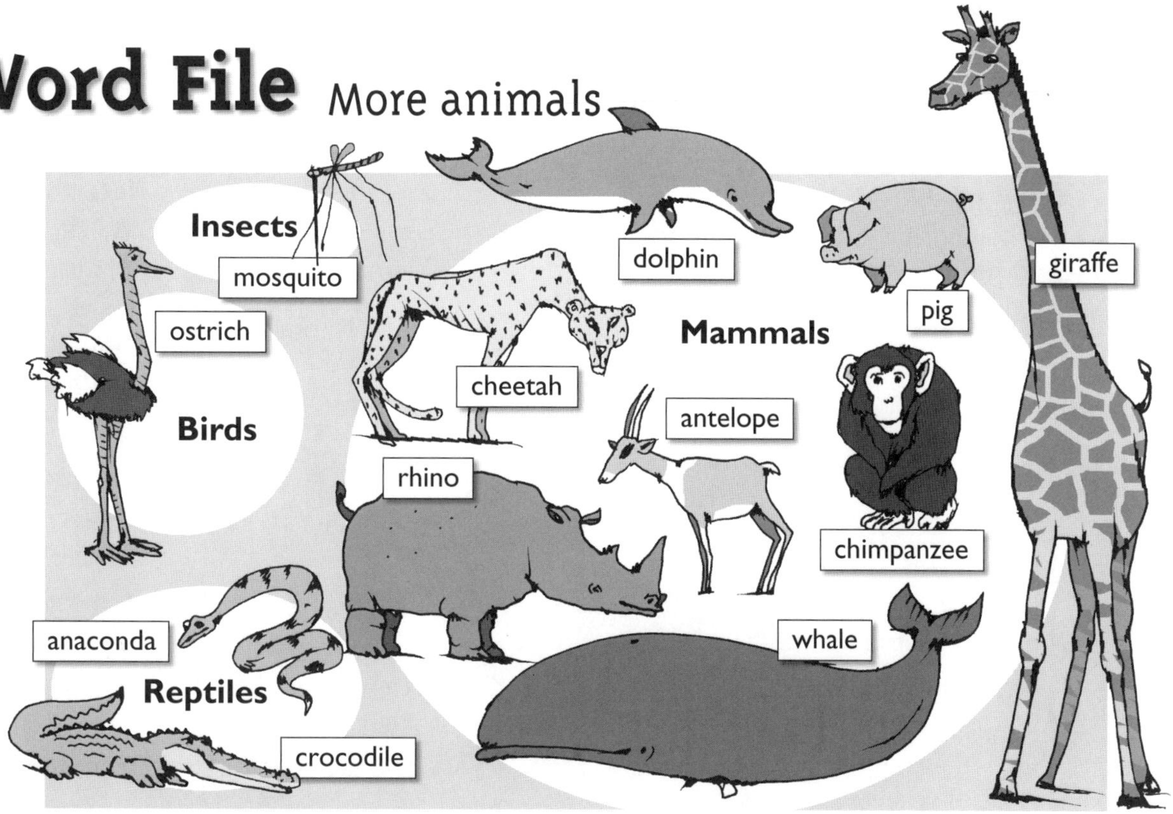

MORE Words and Phrases

1	swimmer	*She is an amazing swimmer.*	Schwimmer/in
	towel	*Have you got a dry towel?*	Handtuch
	middle	*This towel is wet in the middle.*	Mitte
	heavy	*This bag is a bit heavy.*	schwer
	safe	*Is it safe to swim here?*	sicher
	all the time	*It rains all the time in winter.*	die ganze Zeit
	deep	*The water is deep there.*	tief
	in trouble	*He was in trouble – he couldn't swim!*	in Schwierigkeiten sein
	turn around	*When she turned around, she saw the pig.*	(sich) umdrehen
2	**fat**	*My dog's too fat; he needs exercise.*	fett
4	weigh	*I weigh about 60 kilos.*	wiegen
	ton		Tonne (1000 Kilo)
	gram	*How many grams are there in a ton?*	Gramm
	tooth	*My tooth hurts.*	Zahn
	meat	*She doesn't eat meat.*	Fleisch
	tummy	*My tummy is full.*	Bauch
6	**mountain**	*Were there mountains in Atlantis?*	Berg
	ugly	*The rhino is an ugly animal.*	hässlich
	friendly	*Dolphins are friendly animals.*	freundlich
	popular	*They are friendly and popular.*	beliebt
9	amazing	*That pig can swim? That's amazing!*	erstaunlich
	desert	*There are no deserts in England.*	Wüste
	carry	*Mosquitoes can carry malaria.*	tragen; hier: übertragen
	(more) **than**	*I am more than happy to do it.*	(mehr) als
	southeast	*The crocodiles of southeast Asia are the longest in the world.*	südost, Südost-
13	**grow**	*The crocodile can grow to 8 metres.*	wachsen
	high	*The giraffe is the tallest animal at nearly 6 metres high.*	hoch, groß
	nearly		fast, beinahe
	almost	*The blue whale weighs almost 150,000 kilogrammes.*	fast
G	**simple**	*Juggling with two balls is simple.*	einfach
DVD	It depends.		Es kommt darauf an.

Show what you know Units 1–5

What I CAN DO in English

This page helps you to find out how well you are doing.
Read the statements and draw symbols.

☺ = I'm good at this ✓ = I can do this with help ☹ = I need to practise this more

Note:
Wenn du im Buch nachschauen willst, dann helfen dir die Seitenzahlen. Das zeigen sie dir an:

Words

- ◯ I can name at least 10 words for school subjects. (1/10)
- ◯ I can complete questions with the missing question words. (1/12)
- ◯ I can name at least 8 key words from the play *Pronto!* (2/14-18)
- ◯ I can name at least 6 words that have to do with Halloween. (4/26)
- ◯ I can name at least 6 amazing animals. (5/35)

Speaking

- ◯ I can ask and answer questions for a survey about school. (1/9)
- ◯ I can ask and answer questions about yesterday. (2/19)
- ◯ I can ask and answer questions about what people like. (3/24)
- ◯ I can do a guessing game about animals. (Unit 5)
- ◯ I can use superlatives to ask and answer questions about animals. (Unit 5)

Reading and listening

- ◯ I can understand the words to the song *Going places* and sing along. (1/8)
- ◯ I can read and understand the information in the grid *A School Internet Project*. (1/9)
- ◯ I can read and understand the story *First day at school*. (1/11)
- ◯ I can read and understand a text about the blue ring octopus. (1/12)
- ◯ I can listen to, read and understand the poem *The furious octopus*. (1/13)
- ◯ I can listen to, read and understand the play *Pronto!* (2/14-18)
- ◯ I can understand the words to *The Inspector Lime song* and sing along. (2/21)
- ◯ I can read and understand short texts. (3/22)
- ◯ I can understand the words to the song *The Halloween Moon* and sing along. (4/26)
- ◯ I can read and understand short texts from a web page. (4/27)
- ◯ I can read and understand the story *Trick or Treat*. (4/28)
- ◯ I can read and understand texts about real and imaginative animals. (5/32, 34, 35)
- ◯ I can understand the words to the song *A mouth as big as a house* and sing along. (5/37)

Writing for my Portfolio

- ◯ I have written a short text about my summer holidays. (1/12)
- ◯ I have written the continuation of a dialogue. (2/21)
- ◯ I have written a dialogue using *why / because*. (3/25)
- ◯ I have written a story or sentences (using *shouldn't*) about Halloween. (4/29)
- ◯ I have written a text describing an imaginative creature. (5/37)

UNIT 6 Where's the post office?

Revision

■ **1 Do the puzzle and find the secret word.**

			1 O	L	D				
			2 H	E	A	V	Y		
3	F	R	I	E	N	D	L	Y	
			4 B	I	G				
			5 C	L	E	V	E	R	
		6 H	E	A	R	Y			
		7 S	T	R	O	N	G		
			8 Y	O	U	N	G		
					9 S	M	A	L	L

1 Somebody who is 83 is really … .
2 I can't carry this bag. It's too … .
3 Everyone likes them because they're very … .
4 The opposite of small
5 The opposite of stupid
6 With lots of hair on the body
7 She can carry three big bags. She's quite … .
8 The opposite of old
9 It's difficult to see the animal because it's so … .

The secret word is ……………………

■ **2 Complete the sentences. Use comparisons with *than*.**

1 Mr Jones is 50. He is 25 years …………………… his son Tom. (old)
2 The book isn't very good – but the film is …………………… the book! (bad)
3 I am 21 years …………………… my mum. (young)
4 This story is boring! The book I read last week was …………………… this one. (good)
5 This T-shirt is only £ 5.50! All the others are …………………… this one. (expensive)
6 Ken always does his English homework first. It's …………………… for him …………………… Maths. (easy)

■ **3 Complete the dialogues. Use the adjective in brackets.**

1 **A** Do you like English or French?
B I like English – it's ……………*easier than*…………… French! (easy)
2 **A** Do you like crocodiles or sharks?
B Sharks – they're …………………… crocodiles. (dangerous)
3 **A** I don't like their new CD.
B No, it's terrible! It's …………………… their last one! (bad)
4 **A** Why did you buy those shoes?
B Because they were …………………… the other ones. (nice)
5 **A** The homework last night was difficult!
B Yes, it was …………………… last week's. (difficult)
6 **A** Do you like volleyball?
B Yes, I do. I think it's …………………… football. (exciting)

END OF REVISION SECTION

4 Where are these people going? Choose from the words in the box.

railway station
police station
post office
tourist office
bank
church
hospital
shopping centre

1 They're going to the shopping centre.

5 They're going to the police station

2 She's going to the railway station

6 They're going to the tourist office

3 They're going to the bank

7 She is going to the hospital

4 He's going to the church

8 He's going to the post office

5 Complete the dialogues with four of the sentences in the box. There are two extra sentences in the box.

Do you see the traffic lights* up there?
Go past the post office and turn left.
Right, straight ahead, then left.
The bank's just round the corner there.
The church is behind the bank.
Where's that?

Dialogue 1

Girl Excuse me, I'm looking for a bank.
Woman That's easy. Go as far as the shopping centre …
Girl 1 Where is that?
Woman Just follow this road. It's on your left. At the shopping centre turn right …
Girl OK, right at the shopping centre.
Woman 2 The bank's just round the corner there.
Girl Thank you.
Woman You're welcome.

Dialogue 2

Man Excuse me, can you tell me the way to the post office?
Woman The post office? Hmm. There's one in Maple Road.
Man Maple Road? How do I get there?
Woman 3 Do you see the traffic lights up there
Man Yes …
Woman Go to the traffic lights*, turn right, go straight ahead and then turn left.
Man 4 Right, straight ahead, then left
Woman That's Maple Road. The post office is right in front of you.
Man Thank you.

Vocabulary: *traffic lights – (Verkehrs) Ampel

► SB p. 43

★ **6** **Look at the map. Read the two texts and draw the routes on your map.**

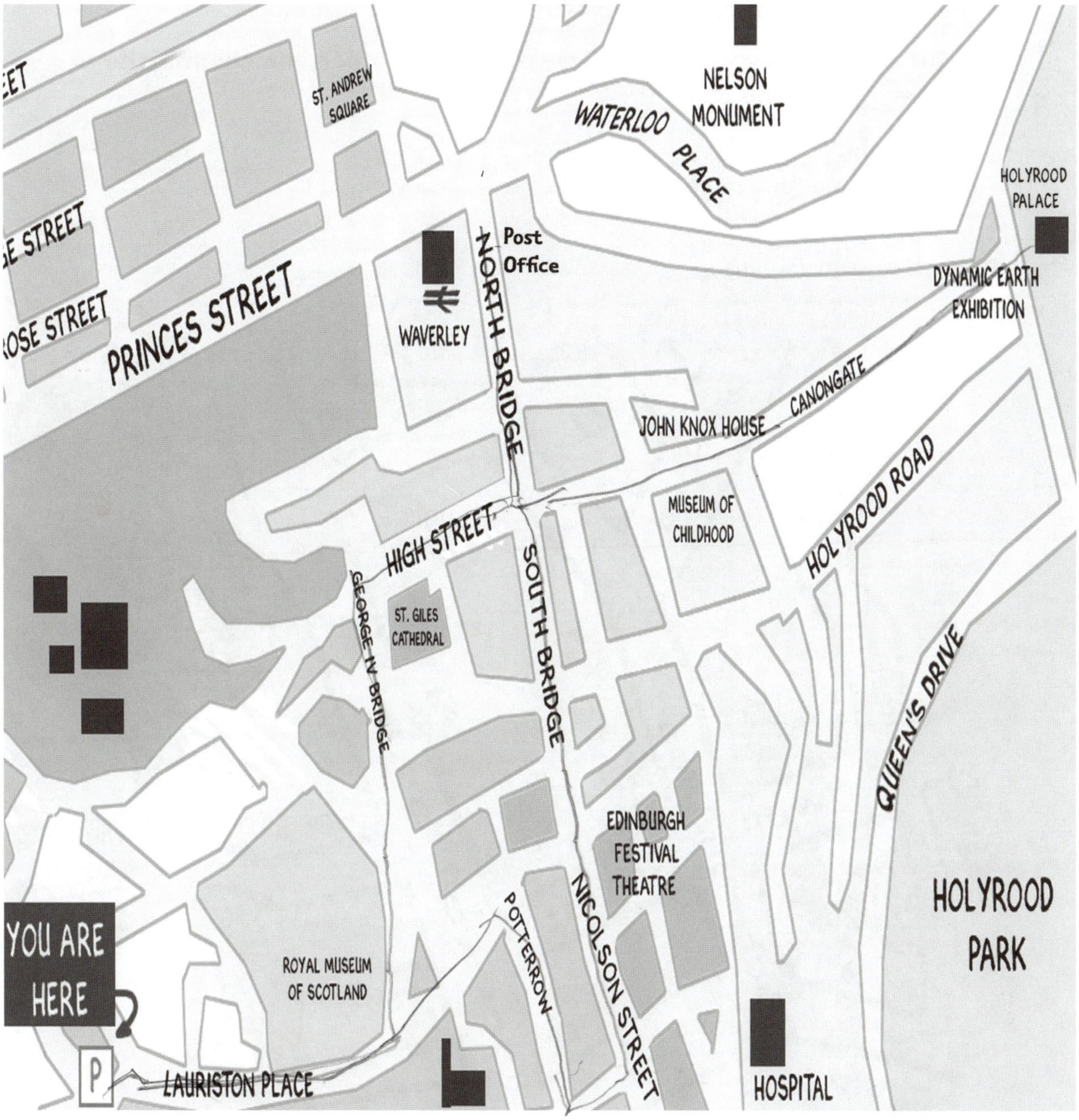

Text 1

From the car park in Lauriston Place to Waverley Station.

Go out of the car park and turn right. Walk down Lauriston Place and turn left at the Royal Museum of Scotland. Walk up George IV Bridge. At St Giles Cathedral turn right into High Street. Go straight on and turn left at North Bridge. Walk down North Bridge as far as the post office. Opposite the post office there is the Waverly station.

Text 2

From the car park in Lauriston Place to Holyrood Palace.

Go out of the car park and turn right. Walk down Lauriston Place. Go straight on into Potterrow; follow it to the right, and then take the first small lane to the left. When you get to Nicolson Street turn left. Go past the Festival Theatre. At the corner of South Bridge and High Street turn right. Go past John Knox House and go straight on Canongate. At the end of Canongate there's Holyrood place.

▶ SB p. 43

■ 7 **Work in pairs. Student B works with the map here. Student A works with the map on page 44 in the Student's Book.**

You ask your partner for the way to the post office, the cinema, the supermarket, the church.

Example:

A *Excuse me, how do I get to the post office? (Excuse me, I'm trying to find … / Excuse me, I'm looking for …)*

B *That's easy. Take the …*

★ 8 **Write a text explaining the way from your home to one of the places below.**

the (nearest) church	the (nearest) cinema	your school
the (nearest) bus station	the (nearest) post office	your favourite shop
the (nearest) supermarket		

....

....

....

....

▶ SB p. 44

Grammar Directions / places

■ **9** **Complete the dialogues with the words in the box.**

cross
ahead
~~straight~~
right
second
turn
take
far

1 **Tourist** Excuse me, where's the railway station?
Policeman Go [1] ......*straight*...... ahead and take the [2] .... right.

2 **Bank robber** Excuse me, where's the nearest bank?
Policeman [3] .... the street and go as [4] .... as the cinema. The bank is next door.

3 **Man** Excuse me, where's the nearest post office?
Policeman [5] .... left, go as far as the cinema and turn [6] ....

4 **Tourist** Excuse me, where's the Chelsea Hotel?
Policeman Go straight [7] .... Go past the shopping centre and [8] .... the first right.

■ **10** **Read the dialogue and circle the correct answer.**

A Excuse me? How do I get to the railway station?
B The railway station? OK. Go [1] *straight down / left* this road. Go [2] *until / as far as* the large supermarket on your left. OK? After the supermarket, [3] *go / take* the second on the right. After about 20 metres, turn [4] *ahead / right* again. Go [5] *past / down* the post office, turn [6] *on / right* at the Station Hotel and there, in front of you, is the railway station. It's a twenty-minute walk.
A Thanks.
B No problem.

★ **11** **Look at the picture. Write sentences using the words in the box.**

next to
behind
opposite
just round the corner
in front of
on the corner of

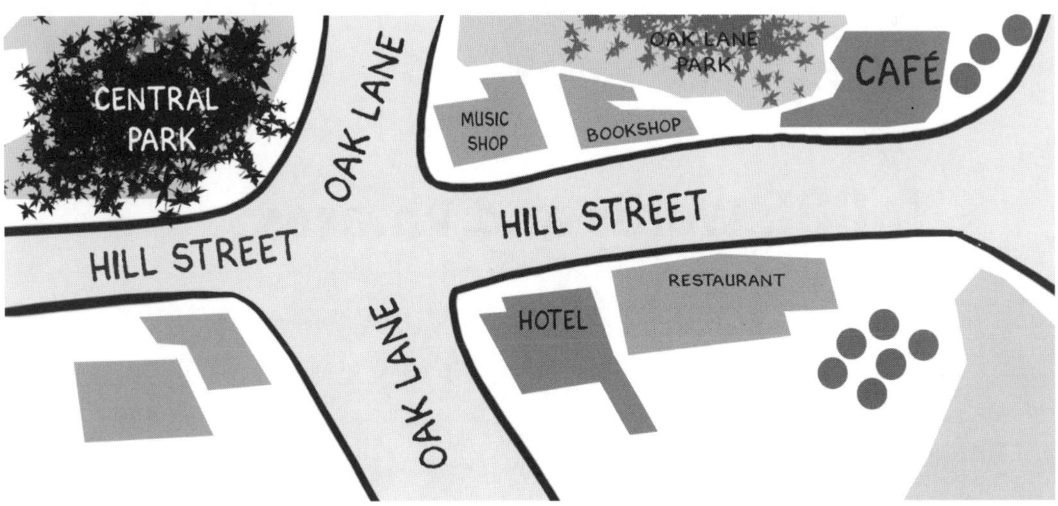

Start like this:

On the corner of Hill Street and Oak Lane there's a music shop. Just round the corner ...

....

....

....

....

▶ SB p. **47**

Word File In a town

How do I get there?

MORE Words and Phrases

1	**forest**		Wald
	path	*This is the best path through the forest.*	Weg, Pfad
	how to	*Do you know how to open it?*	wie man
	luck	*Good luck, sir!*	Glück
3	**as far as**	*Follow the road as far as the supermarket.*	bis zu
	(not) **at all**	*Thank you. – Not at all.*	gar nicht; hier: keine Ursache
	woman (pl women)	*The woman tells the man where the post office is.*	Frau
4	**hill**	*Walk up the hill as far as the church.*	Hügel
6	**stay at**	*When I go to London I stay at my uncle's house.*	übernachten (bei)
	classmate	*Meet my classmate, Betty.*	Klassenkamerad/in, Mitschüler/in
	sign	*There's a no entry sign at the end of our road.*	Zeichen, Schild
	low	*The battery in my mobile is low.*	niedrig, schwach
	main	*The main street is called Oxford Street.*	Haupt-
	put on	*I put on my jacket and go to my bike.*	anziehen
7	**phone call**	*George got a phone call from Danielle.*	Telefonanruf

UNIT 7 Outdoor adventure

Revision

1 Where can you find these things? Write the name of the places next to the pictures.

~~police station~~	~~church~~
~~tourist office~~	~~railway station~~
~~post office~~	~~hospital~~
~~bank~~	~~shopping centre~~

1 post office

2 church

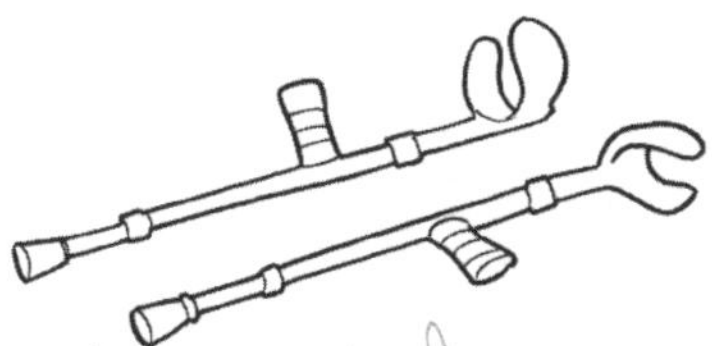

3 hospital

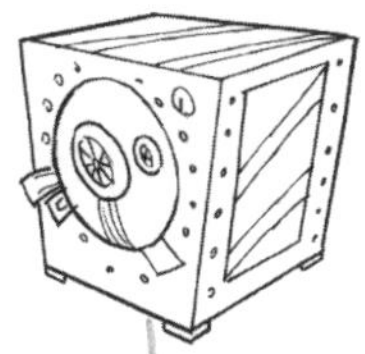

4 bank

5 Police station

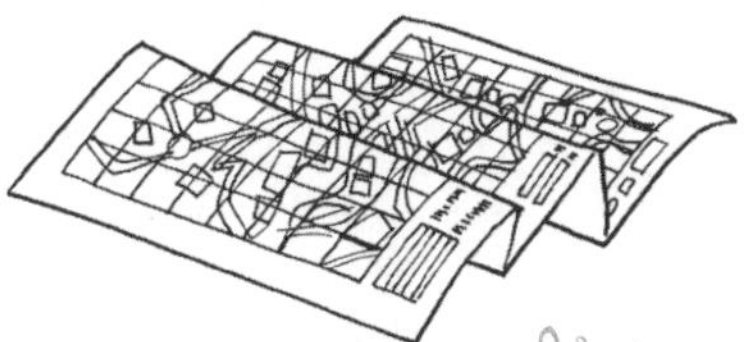

6 tourist office

7 shopping centre

8 railway station

2 Write the sentences under the pictures.

~~It's next to the bank.~~ ~~It's just round the corner.~~ ~~Cross the road.~~
~~It's behind the bank.~~ ~~Go straight ahead.~~ ~~Go past the bank.~~
~~Take the third right.~~ ~~It's opposite the bank.~~

1 Go past the bank

2 Go straight ahead

3 It's opposite to the bank

4 It's next to the bank

5 It's just round the corner

6 Take the third right

7 Cross the road

8 It's behind the bank

END OF REVISION SECTION

3 Look at the pictures. Write the numbers next to the words in the box.

- ☐ hills
- ☐ stars
- ☐ a mountain
- ☐ a lake
- ☐ a road
- ☐ a field
- ☐ a beach
- ☐ the sea
- ☐ the sun
- ☐ the moon
- ☐ a forest
- ☐ a river

Picture 1

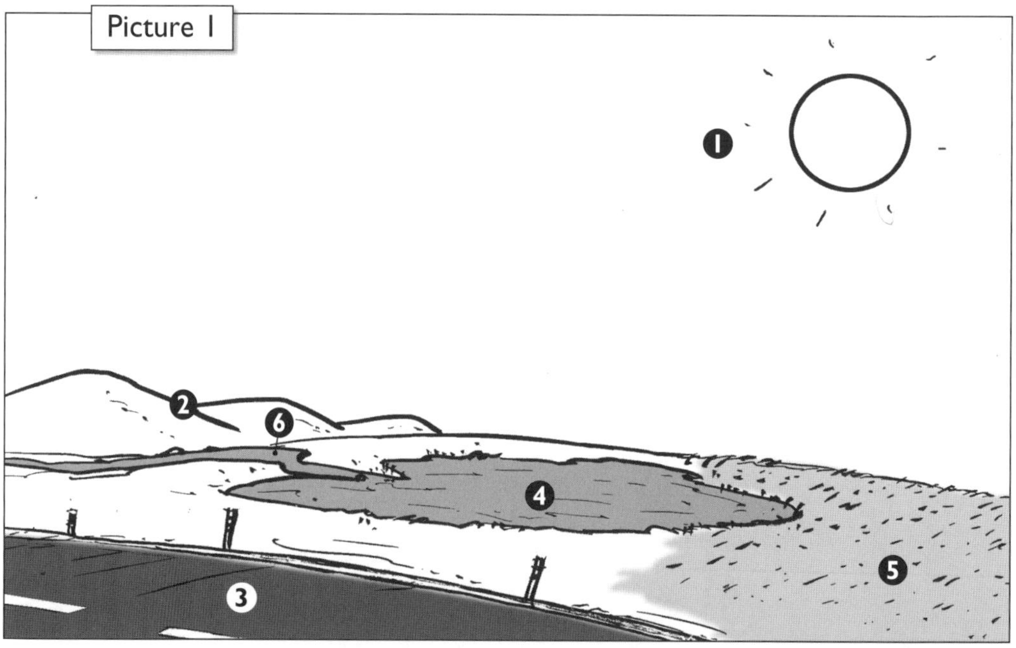

Picture 2

★ **4 Cover the pictures. How much can you remember? Circle T (*True*) or F (*False*). Look and check.**

Picture 1

1 The sun is in the top right-hand corner of the picture. T / F
2 The road is in the top left-hand corner of the picture. T / F
3 The lake is in the middle of the picture. T / F
4 The fields are on the left-hand side of the picture. T / F

Picture 2

5 The moon is in the top right-hand corner of the picture. T / F
6 The forest is on the right-hand side of the picture. T / F
7 The mountain is in the top left-hand corner of the picture. T / F
8 The mountain is next to the moon. T / F

▶ SB p. 48

● 5 Match the pictures with the sentences.

1 They're canoeing on a river.
2 They're swimming next to a waterfall.
3 They're having a picnic.
4 They're rock climbing.
5 They're building a tree house.
6 They're geo-caching.

a

b

c

d

e

f

■ 6 Put the dialogue in the correct order.

Let's go rock climbing.

- Tuesday 3 p.m.
- Wear warm clothes and a good pair of boots.
- Wear a hard hat all the time!

Vocabulary: *boot – Stiefel

- [ ] **B** Of course. I know that.
- [ ] **B** Rock climbing? I'm not sure.
- [ ] **B** Everyone? Oh, alright. I hope it's fun.
- [ ] **A** Oh, come on. Everyone's going.
- [1] **A** Let's go rock climbing tomorrow.
- [ ] **A** Great. But bring some warm clothes and a good pair of boots*. And you have to wear a hard hat all the time.

★ 7 Write similar dialogues for these signs in your exercise book.

Let's go and build a tree house.

- Monday 10 a.m.
- Get a hard hat from the office and wear it all the time.

Let's go on a Picnic.

- Wednesday 1 p.m.
- Bring your own food.
- Free cola and orange juice
- Don't forget to clean up the picnic area after the picnic.

▶ SB p. 49

★ **8** **Read the summary of *Treasure Hunt* on page 50 of the Student's Book. There are four extra sentences.**

1 Chris went to an adventure holiday camp with his twelve-year-old sister Gillie.
2 Chris thought the camp was great.
3 Their parents phoned them every night.
4 The guides were great and Chris especially liked one called Ron.
5 One Wednesday Chris, Gillie and some more kids went geo-caching.
6 Gillie found something in a hole.
7 It wasn't the cache. It was some old coins.
8 Ron gave them some treats and took the coins.
9 That evening they watched a film about a bank robber.
10 Two days later they went to a museum.
11 The weather was very bad and they didn't have an umbrella.
12 They saw lots of old Roman coins.
13 They were the same as the coins Gillie found.
14 There was a man in a uniform in the museum. Gillie told him about her coins.
15 Ron ran away and the man called the police.
16 The man ate a big sandwich.
17 Two days later the police found Ron and took the coins off him.
18 Now the coins are in the museum with a sign. It says "Coins found by Gillie Woodhouse."

■ **9** **Read the story and put the pictures in order.**

One day I went geo-caching with two of my friends, Charlie and Sue. I didn't know what geo-caching was but Sue told me everything. I liked the idea. What a good idea for a hot Sunday morning!

We met at Sue's house. We turned on Sue's GPS and put in the coordinates. A little red sign on the GPS showed us the way to go and we started walking. We walked down the road and out of the town. We walked through some fields and we then walked up and down two hills. We were tired, hot and hungry. Nobody had any food. Should we go on? We looked down at the GPS. Only one more kilometre. We didn't want to stop now.

Fifteen minutes later, we arrived at a forest. It was large and very dark inside. Charlie was a bit scared. So was I, but I didn't say anything. Should we go in? We looked down at the GPS. Only 500 m more. We had to go on.

Ten minutes later, we came to a river. It was quite big and there wasn't a bridge. Should we cross it? We looked down at the GPS. Only 50 m! We all jumped into the river and swam to the opposite side.

We got out of the river. The GPS showed us that the treasure was under our feet. We looked down and saw a hole in the ground. Sue put in her hand and pulled out a box. We were all very excited. We opened the box and …

★ **10** **Write two or three sentences to complete the story in your exercise book.**

▶ SB pp. 50, 51

Grammar *have to*

● **11 Look at the signs and circle the correct answer.**

1 You *have to* / *don't have to* be 18 or older to get into the disco.
2 You *have to* / *don't have to* turn off your mobile phone in the cinema.
3 You *have to* / *don't have to* buy a ticket for the zoo on Sundays.
4 We *have to* / *don't have to* wear our school uniform this Friday.
5 You *have to* / *don't have to* be quiet after 10 p.m.
6 You *have to* / *don't have to* be taller than 1 metre to go on the ride.

■ **12 Complete the sentences with the correct form of *(not) have to* and the words in the box.**

invite
do
study*
take
go
run
~~eat~~
be

1 **A** I'm really not very hungry.
B Well, you ......don't have to eat...... everything.
2 **A** Can you help me make dinner?
B I'm sorry but I .... my homework.
3 **A** I think there is a problem with your laptop.
B I know. I .... it to the shop.
4 **A** The bus leaves at 3 p.m. We've got lots of time.
B Good. So we ....
5 **A** We've got a big test tomorrow.
B Yeah. I .... a lot tonight.
6 **A** I don't really like Colin Wood.
B Well it's your party. You .... him.
7 **A** Where's mum?
B Her head hurts. She's in bed so you .... quiet.
8 **A** Don't forget you've got to see the doctor after school.
B But I don't feel ill any more so I ....

● **13 Tick the sentences that are true for you.**

Vocabulary: *study – lernen, studieren

1 I have to do a lot of homework tonight. ☐
2 I have to see my whole family this weekend. ☐
3 I don't have to go to school tomorrow. ☐
4 I don't have to help my mum and dad in the house. ☐
5 I have to go to the dentist's soon. ☐
6 I don't have to go to bed early tonight. ☐
7 I have to study* for a test this week. ☐
8 I have to get up at 6 a.m. Mondays to Fridays. ☐

▶ SB p. 53

Word File

Landscape

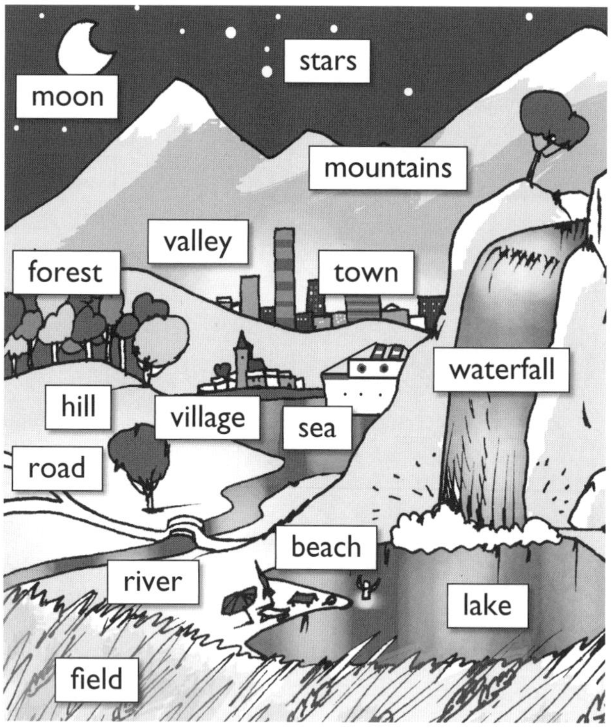

On holiday

MORE Words and Phrases

2	right-hand	*On the right-hand side there's a waterfall.*	rechte(r, s)
	left-hand	*On the left-hand side there's a lake.*	linke(r, s)
	bottom	*It's in the bottom right-hand corner of the picture.*	unten
3	**all the time**	*It rains all the time in winter.*	die ganze Zeit
	area	*The picnic area was large.*	Gebiet, Region, Platz
	build	*Let's build a bridge.*	bauen
	wait a minute	*Wait a minute, I think I'll join you.*	warte mal; einen Moment
5	**move**	*We moved to Munich.*	hier: umziehen
6	**after all**	*Franz speaks good English – after all, he lives in London.*	schließlich
	any more	*We couldn't find the ring any more.*	nicht mehr
	go along	*I went along too.*	mitgehen
	so-called	*The treasure is a small box, the so-called "cache".*	sogenannt/e, er, es
7	most of the time	*It rains most of the time in summer, too.*	meistens
	especially	*I'm always tired, especially in the morning.*	besonders
	list	*Please make a list.*	Liste
	note	*Write me a note, please.*	Notiz
	bottle	*I take a bottle of water in my bag.*	Flasche
	find out	*Let's find out what's under this rock!*	herausfinden
	unit	*You need a GPS unit.*	Gerät, Einheit
	for example	*Have you got a pet? A dog, for example?*	zum Beispiel
	something else	*There's something else in here!*	noch etwas
	several		einige, mehrere
	coin	*I have several coins.*	Münze, Geldstück
	joke	*That's a joke – these coins are plastic!*	Witz
	exactly	*That's exactly right.*	genau
	point (at)	*Please point at what you like.*	zeigen (auf)
8	take part	*Gillie and Chris took part in a treasure hunt.*	teilnehmen

UNIT 8 We might go out

Revision

● ① **Find the wrong word.**

1 stars beach moon sun
2 river lake field sea
3 mountain forest hills moon
4 river road motorway street
5 village valley city town

★ ② **Read the signs at an adventure camp. Write 1, 2, 3 or 4 next to the sentences.**

1 It's at the weekend. ☐
2 You have to talk to your mother and father first. ☐
3 It starts at the bottom of a mountain. ☐
4 You have to arrive before 2 p.m. 4
5 You have to wear a jacket. ☐
6 You have to wear a hat and a life jacket. ☐
7 You have to take things to eat. ☐
8 You have to get up early. ☐

❸

❶

❹

❷

Vocabulary: *permission – Erlaubnis

● ③ **Complete with *have to* or *don't have to*.**

1 Tomorrow's Sunday so we .... go to school.
2 I'm sorry, I can't talk to you now. I .... finish my homework.
3 It's free! You .... buy a ticket.
4 We .... study this weekend because there's a test next week.

END OF REVISION SECTION

● 4 Look at the pictures and complete the sentences with the words in the box.

doing
playing
staying
watching
having
tidying
doing
doing

1 Peter is ....watching.... a DVD.

2 Bob is ....doing.... the shopping.

3 Sue is ....tidying.... her room.

4 Mike is ....playing.... volleyball.

5 Steve is ....doing.... his homework.

6 Abi is ....staying.... at a friend's house.

7 Jane is ....having.... a party.

8 Ron is ....doing.... nothing.

■ 5 Choose the correct answers about the sketch *On Strike* on page 56 of the Student's Book. Then read the sketch again and check.

1 Why do Simon and Sally go on strike?
- [ ] a) They want more money.
- [x] b) There's too much work for them.
- [ ] c) They don't want to go to school.

2 What does Sally say that she is not going to do?
- [x] a) Tidy her room.
- [ ] b) Put the rubbish out.
- [ ] c) Do the shopping.

3 What does Simon say he's not going to do?
- [ ] a) Do the washing-up.
- [ ] b) Tidy his room.
- [x] c) Put the rubbish out.

4 What do their parents think about their strike?
- [x] a) It's OK for them.
- [ ] b) They're angry.
- [ ] c) They think it's funny.

5 What does Sally want her mum to do?
- [ ] a) Help her with her homework.
- [ ] b) Go shopping with her.
- [x] c) Make breakfast for her.

6 What does Simon want his dad to do?
- [x] a) Take him to his football match.
- [ ] b) Play football with him.
- [ ] c) Buy him some football shoes.

▶ SB p. 56

6 Complete the dialogue with the words in the box.

~~shopping~~
~~tidy~~
~~tired~~
~~take~~
~~isn't~~
~~going~~
~~to~~
~~do~~

Cathy Dad, can Olivia and I go to the party tonight?

Dad What does your mum think?

James She doesn't know.

Olivia We're [1] going to ask her when she gets home.

Dad Well. OK, but you have to tidy the house first.

Cathy What? All of it?

Dad Well, you can both start with the living room.

Olivia The living room!

Dad Yes. And then you can [2] do your bedrooms.

James Ha, ha.

Cathy No problem. My bedroom's always tidy.

Dad So you can help me do the [3] shopping

Olivia Ha, ha.

Dad And you have to [4] take the rubbish out.

Olivia Dad!

James It's going [5] to be a nice quiet afternoon for me.

Dad No, it [6] isn't ! You're going to [7] tidy the washing-up.

Olivia Ha, ha.

Dad So – come on, everyone. Let's get busy.

(Three hours later.)

Dad That was quite a lot of work.

Olivia Yes, it was. I'm really [8] tired .

Cathy Me too.

James Mum's home.

Mum Hello everyone. Wow, the house is so tidy. That's great. Because …

Olivia Because what?

Mum Because we're having guests here for dinner tonight.

Olivia Oh no!

7 Who's going to do what? Write *Dad*, *James*, *Olivia* or *Cathy* under the pictures.

1 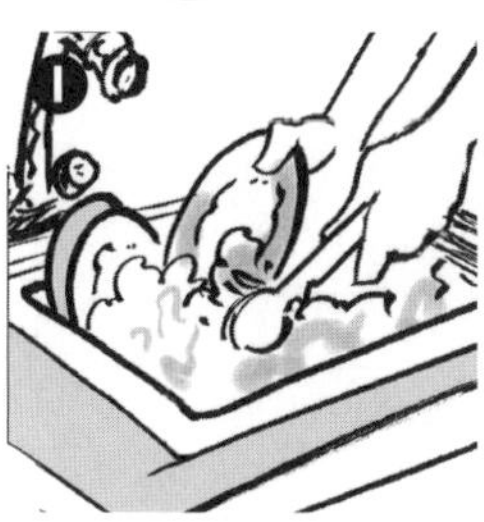
....

2 
....

3 
....

4 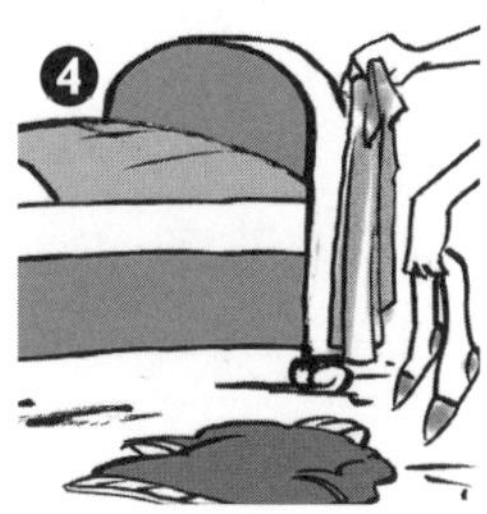
....

5 
....

8 Write sentences about what everyone is going to do.

Example: *James is going to do the washing-up.*

....

....

....

....

SB p. **56**

★ **9** **Read the story and complete with the expressions in the box.**

William the worrier

Don What's the matter, William? Are you sad?
William No, I'm not sad. I'm sick.
Don Sick? What did you eat?
William No, I'm love sick.
Don Love sick?
William Yes, love sick. I'm in love with Katy Pimm but she doesn't even know my name.

make her ill
get it
like films
red and feel ill
like you better than me
be allergic* to them

Don You have to talk to her. It's easy.
William Good idea, but there's one problem. I'm too shy*. I might go 1 ....
Don Well, send her a letter.
William That isn't a very good idea. She might not 2 ....
Don OK, then. Let me talk to her for you.
William No! No way! She might 3 .... !

Don Invite her to the cinema.
William No. She might not 4 ....
Don Oh, come on.
William But she might say "No".
Don Send her some flowers.
William That's not a good idea. She might 5 ....

Don I know! Do something romantic. Give her some chocolates.
William No, no. They might 6 .... That's not a good idea.
Don I give up.*

Don Look. Katy's walking towards us.
William Is she? Quick – let's hide!
Don Too late. Hi Katy.
Katy Hi Don. Hello William. I'm Katy.
William Er ... hello.
Katy Hi. Would you like to come to the cinema tonight?

Vocabulary: *shy – schüchtern / allergic – allergisch / give up – aufgeben

▶ SB p. 57

Grammar *going to* – negative

● 10 **Write the letters of the pictures next to the sentences.**

1 They aren't going to catch the bus. ☐
2 They're going to catch a bus. ☐
3 She's going to win. ☐
4 She isn't going to win. ☐
5 They're going to have fish for lunch. ☐
6 They aren't going to have fish for lunch. ☐

■ 11 **Complete the sentences with *not going to* and the verb from the question.**

1 **A** Are you going to invite Ben to your party?
B Yes, but ......I'm not going to invite...... his brother.

2 **A** Are you going to do your English homework tonight?
B Yes, but .... all of it.

3 **A** Is he going to tidy his room?
B Yes, but .... the living room.

4 **A** Is she going to tell her mum?
B Yes, but .... her dad.

5 **A** Are we going to have chicken for lunch?
B Yes, but .... it with chips.

6 **A** Are they going to do the washing-up?
B Yes, but .... the shopping.

Grammar *might*

■ 12 **Match to make sentences.**

1 It might rain	☐	and she might say 'yes'.
2 My head hurts	☐	and she might buy their new CD.
3 I need a new shirt	☐	so I might take an aspirin.
4 She quite likes U2	☐	so I might go shopping tomorrow.
5 He drank a lot of coffee	☐	so she's going to take an umbrella.
6 He asked her to be his wife	☐	so he might not sleep well tonight.

▶ SB p. 59

Word File Helping at home

MORE Words and Phrases

1	tidy	*I don't want to tidy my room today, but I will do it tomorrow.*	aufräumen
2	**invite**	*I invited some friends to a party.*	einladen
7	on strike	*I'm on strike! I'm not going to work any more.*	im Streik
	rubbish	*They collect the rubbish from our street on Thursdays.*	Müll
	bacon	*Bacon and eggs is a traditional English breakfast.*	Speck
	Pardon	*Pardon? I didn't hear you.*	Entschuldigung!, wie bitte?
9	**drive**	*Can you drive that car?*	fahren
	be worried	*I'm worried because my dog is very ill.*	sich Sorgen machen
	practice	*Practice makes perfect.*	Übung
	might	*I might go shopping tomorrow if I have time.*	könnte; vielleicht (tun, sein)
	crash	*I didn't crash, did I?*	zu Bruch fahren
10	**study**	*We have to study hard for our exams.*	studieren; lernen
13	get into trouble	*I might get into trouble if I do that.*	in Schwierigkeiten geraten, Ärger bekommen
	fancy dress	*What are you wearing for the fancy dress party?*	Verkleidung, Kostüm
	finish	*The party finishes at half past twelve.*	beenden, vervollständigen

Strange things from space!

Revision

● 1 **Use the pictures to write sentences.**

The things Alison did last weekend.

1 She watched 3 DVDs.

2 ....

3 ....

4 ....

5 ....

6 ....

And this weekend, she wants to do nothing at all!

● 2 **Put the dialogue in the correct order.**

☐ **Tim** OK. I'm going to phone Ben. He might want to come.
☐ **Tim** I'm not sure. I might go shopping.
☐ **Tim** I like shopping. What about you? What are you going to do?
1 **Rebecca** What are you going to do this weekend?
☐ **Rebecca** Nothing special. But I'm not going shopping, for sure.
☐ **Rebecca** Shopping! Haven't you got anything better to do?
☐ **Rebecca** Shopping with Ben! Hmm. I think I might come. I need some new jeans.

★ 3 **Write Tim's phone call with Ben.**

Tim Hi Ben, what are you going to do this weekend?
Ben I'm not sure. I might ....
Tim ....
Ben ....
Tim ....

● 4 **Tick the sentences that are true for you.**

1 I'm going to learn to drive when I'm 18. ☐
2 I'm not going to be very rich. ☐
3 I'm not going to live in another country. ☐
4 I'm going to be a doctor. ☐
5 I'm going to be famous. ☐
6 I'm not going to have a car. ☐

END OF REVISION SECTION

5 Put the summary of *A new home* into the correct order.

- [ ] Jenny's father got in his car and left. Jenny started tidying up. She got a broom to sweep up the seeds. Then she put them into the dustbin.
- [ ] When all the spaceships were ready, the Trojans left for the planet Earth. And twenty years later they arrived there.
- [1] The president of Trojan asked her people to build 20,000 spaceships, because they had to leave their planet.
- [ ] Her father came out of the house and saw the seeds, too. He walked on some of the seeds and they went 'crack!'.
- [ ] On Earth, Jenny was in her garden. Suddenly she saw thousands of round yellow seeds falling from the sky.
- [ ] With 20,000 spaceships (each could carry 10,000 Trojans) they could all go to a safe place before the other planet hit them.

6 Read the text and put the pictures in the correct order.

1 Most of the spaceships landed in Jenny's garden.
2 Some landed near a little lake in the woods.
3 The Trojans built a palace* near the lake.
4 Sometimes people walked past the lake.
5 One day a boy with binoculars* looked at the place and saw the Trojans.
6 The next day, newspaper reporters came from all over* the world.

Vocabulary:
*palace – Palast / binoculars – Fernglas
from all over – von überall her

▶ SB p. 62

7 Complete the dialogue with sentences in the box.

Are you going to France, too?

They're in the fridge.

Where are you going this time?

Yes, there was.

You know I love them.

Time traveller's wife	Are you leaving again, dear?
Time traveller*	Yes I am, dear.
Time traveller's wife	1 ....
Time traveller	To England, 1066.
Time traveller's wife	Oh, wasn't there a big battle* in 1066?
Time traveller	2 ....
Time traveller's wife	Can you bring back a present for Jonathan? It's his birthday next week.
Time traveller	OK. Anything else?
Time traveller's wife	Not from England. 3 ....
Time traveller	Maybe. Around 1900.
Time traveller's wife	Oh, good. Bring back some cheese for the party on Sunday. And dear?
Time traveller	Yes?
Time traveller's wife	Don't forget the Sachertortes for breakfast. 4 ....
Time traveller	We don't need Sachertortes. I got three yesterday. 5 ....
Time traveller's wife	Oh. OK. Thanks. Now hurry, or you'll miss the battle in 1066!

Vocabulary:
*time traveller – Zeitreisende/r
battle – Schlacht

8 Circle T (*True*) or F (*False*).

1 The time traveller is going to the year 1066. T / F
2 He's going there because it's his birthday next week. T / F
3 Then he's going to England in 1900. T / F
4 His wife wants some cheese for the party on Sunday. T / F
5 He's going to get some Sachertortes. T / F

★ 9 Read the text and complete with the time expressions in the box.

The next moment

Three days later

At first

yesterday

suddenly

The next morning

James went into the house. He didn't see anything special in the living room, so he went upstairs to a bedroom. He looked around, and 1 .... , he saw a big book on the bed. He opened it and started to read. There were lots of stories about life on other planets. In the book he found a picture of a spaceship. James saw that there was a telephone number on the back of the book. 2 .... , James didn't know what to do. But then he picked up the phone and called the number. Somebody answered, but James didn't understand a word. James got into bed and slept all night. 3 .... , he woke up and heard a strange noise. He went to the window and looked out. There he saw the spaceship from the book. 4 .... , the door to the spaceship opened and a strange creature came out. "You called us 5 ....!" the creature said. "Come with us!" 6 .... , James was on another planet!

SB p. 63

Grammar Past simple / past time markers

● **10** **Find the ten verbs and write them in the past simple. Look in all directions.**

S	C	O	M	E	T	W	H
T	P	O	F	I	N	D	C
A	L	U	S	B	N	T	I
R	S	I	T	S	A	N	T
T	V	Q	R	K	L	R	A
T	R	O	Y	Z	P	R	K
U	D	L	I	U	B	O	E
N	U	S	T	O	P	H	S

came
....
....
....
....
....
....
....
....
....

■ **11** **Write the verbs in brackets in the past simple.**

A month ago I 1.................... (watch) a science fiction film about aliens. They 2.................... (look) like us, they had jobs like us, they had lives just like us. But they gave commands. The aliens were the bosses*, and we were servants. They 3.................... (send) messages through TV, and when people were almost sleeping in front of their TVs, the messages were always there. With the help of special glasses, you 4.................... (know) who was an alien. One day a man 5.................... (find) a pair of these glasses, and he 6.................... (start) fighting the aliens. It was an old film, but I 7.................... (like) it a lot.

Vocabulary: *boss – Chef

● **12** **What happened to Natasha? Put the sentences in the correct order.**

☐ An hour later, the car turned into a spaceship.
☐ She liked him and after two days she fell in love with* him.
☐ Ten hours later they were in the young man's home town on THX-15.
1 A month ago, Natasha met a young man.
☐ Three days ago he invited her to his home town.
☐ Yesterday they left the city in his car.
☐ Now Natasha is on planet THX-15.

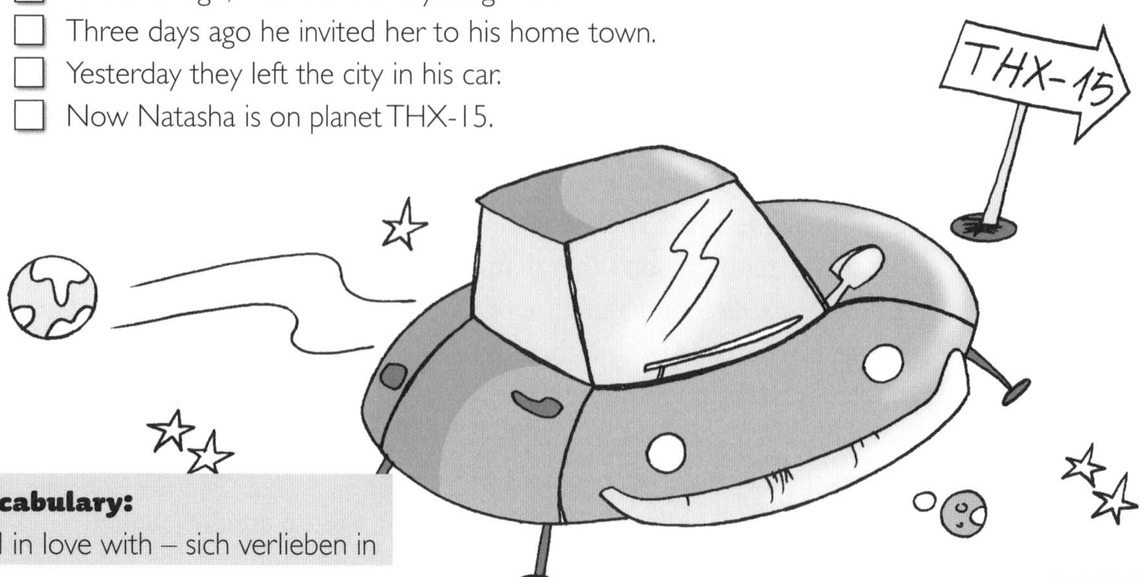

Vocabulary:
*fall in love with – sich verlieben in

▶ SB p. 65

13 Look at the picture story. Put the sentences in the correct order.

[ ] A week later, my brother was at the desk in his room again.
[ ] Five years later the dinosaur was as big as our house.
[ ] He opened the box to look at the egg.
[ ] He picked the egg up and took it to his room.
[ ] He put it in a box near the central heating* to keep it warm.
[1] Five years ago, my brother found an egg behind a bush in our garden.
[ ] Suddenly he heard a noise, but he didn't know what it was.
[ ] The next day he heard the noise again.
[ ] There was no egg any more, but a little dinosaur.

Vocabulary: *central heating – Zentralheizung

★ 14 Write sentences that are true for you.

1 Two weeks ago ....
2 Last week ....
3 Yesterday ....
4 Five hours ago ....
5 At ten past eight this morning ....
....

▶ SB p. 65

Word File

To the stars

MORE Words and Phrases

2	**photograph**	*It takes good photographs.*	Foto(grafie)
3	**Earth**	*The spaceships landed on Earth.*	Erde
	get ready	*Now, we have to get ready.*	sich fertig machen für
	it takes	*It took them a long time to build the spaceships.*	man braucht
	one by one	*One by one, the spaceships took off.*	einer nach dem anderen
	huge	*His spaceship is huge.*	riesig, riesengroß
	journey	*They went on a long journey to visit their cousins.*	Reise
4	**travel**	*I'd like to travel the world.*	reisen, bereisen
	plan	*The people planned very big spaceships.*	planen
5	bark	*The dog barked at the tree.*	bellen
	round	*The ball is round.*	rund
	seed	*The seeds are yellow.*	Same(n)
	broom		Besen
	sweep	*Please sweep the floor with this broom.*	kehren
	dustbin	*Put all the rubbish in the dustbin.*	Mülleimer
10	**light**	*There was a green light in a window.*	Licht
12	**comfortable**	*This chair is very comfortable.*	bequem
	button	*If you push this button, the machine comes on.*	Knopf

UNIT 10 Are you ready to order?

Revision

■ 1 **Put the sentences of the story in the correct order.**

☐ After fifteen minutes, I went to talk to the cinema manager, but she didn't have it.
1 Yesterday, I lost my wallet in the cinema.
☐ I walked back to the cinema again.
☐ After two hours I got home, tired and unhappy.
☐ I looked in the cinema for it, but I didn't find it.
☐ Finally, I got my wallet back. And I was lucky – my money was still there!
☐ A few minutes later, the cinema manager phoned me. 'Someone found your wallet,' she said.
☐ Then I walked home because I didn't have the money for a bus ticket.

● 2 **Write the verbs in brackets in the past simple.**

1 We .... (go) into the cinema and .... (sit) down.
2 The film .... (start) at eight o'clock.
3 We .... (enjoy) the film a lot.
4 After the film we .... (have) a pizza.
5 Finally, my dad .... (come) in his car.
6 He .... (take) us home.

■ 3 **Write the questions.**

1 **A** *Where did you go last night?*
B I went to the cinema.

2 **A** .... with?
B I went with Martin and Annie.

3 **A** .... ?
B A new adventure film.

4 **A** .... ?
B Yes, I really enjoyed it.

5 **A** .... after the cinema?
B We went for a pizza.

6 **A** .... ?
B Charlie's Pizza House.

7 **A** .... ?
B I had a cheese and tomato pizza.

8 **A** .... ?
B I got home about 8 p.m.

END OF REVISION SECTION

4 **Do the crossword.**

Down:

Across:

5 **Read the menu and write the names of the pizzas under the pictures. There are two extra names.**

Pisa
peas, onions, red peppers, cheese

Turin
egg, broccoli, onions, red peppers, cheese

Rome
sausage, tomatoes, onions, broccoli, cheese

Naples
egg, tomatoes, broccoli, peas, red peppers, cheese

Florence
tomatoes, cheese

Milan
sausage, peas, tomatoes, cheese

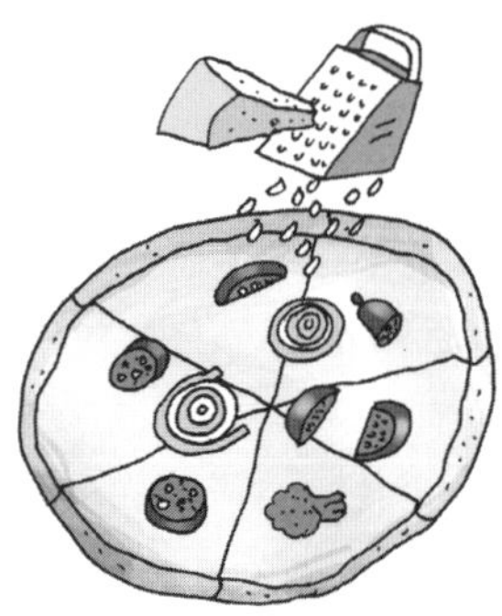

ROME

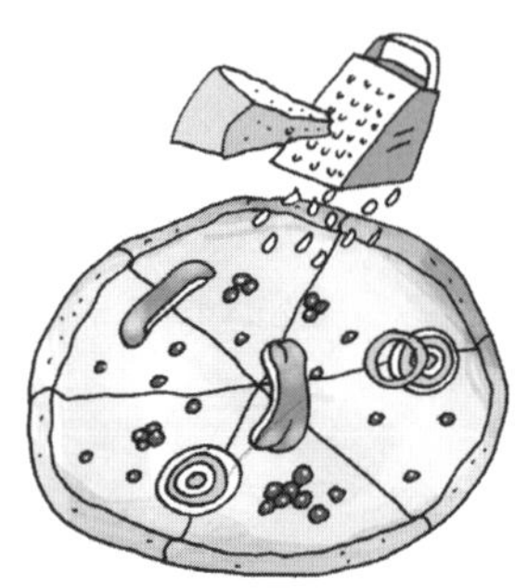

PISA

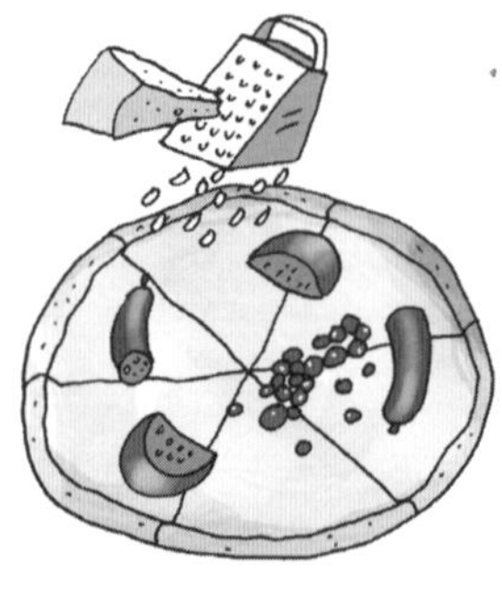

Milan

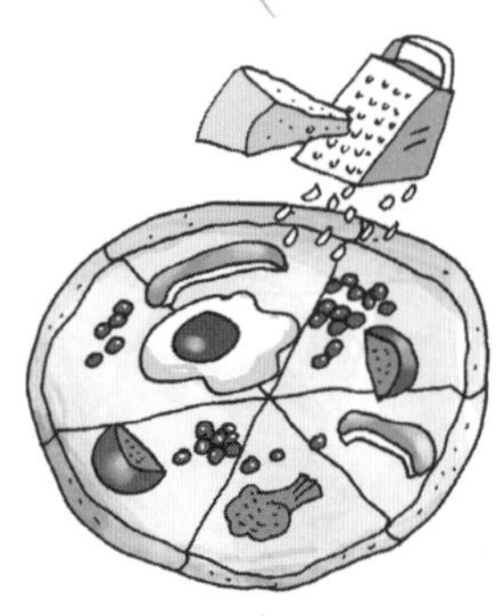

Naples

SB p. 67

■ **6** **Put the dialogue in the correct order.**

☐ **Customer*** No thanks. I don't like olives.
☐ **Customer** That's right.
☐ **Customer** Yes. I'd like a Rome pizza, please. But I don't want any onions.
☐ **Customer** Water, please. A bottle of mineral water.
☐ **Waiter** OK. No onions. Would you like olives maybe?
1 **Waiter** Are you ready to order?
☐ **Waiter** Thank you. I'll bring the water straightaway.
☐ **Waiter** OK. A Rome pizza, no onions, and a mineral water.
☐ **Waiter** OK – no olives and no onions. And what would you like to drink?

Vocabulary:
*customer – Kunde, Kundin; Gast

■ **7** **Write the waiter's questions to complete the dialogue.**

Waiter 1 .... ?
Customer* Yes. I'd like a Milan pizza, please. But I don't want any peas.
Waiter 2 .... ?
Customer No thanks. I don't like peppers.
Waiter OK – no peppers. 3 .... ?
Customer A cola please.
Waiter One cola, coming straightaway. 4 .... ?
Customer Not now, but I might order an ice cream later.
Waiter No problem.

★ **8** **Write a dialogue between a waiter and a customer* in your exercise book.**

The customer wants …
a Turin pizza, but with no egg | an orange juice | some chocolate cake

★ **9** **Look at the picture of the sketch *The best restaurant in town*. Can you find four mistakes? The first one is done for you. Write down the other three and then look at Student's Book page 68 to check.**

Example:

They didn't go with their son.

....

....

....

....

....

....

....

▶ SB p. 69

★ **10** **Read the summary of *The best restaurant in town* and write the numbers of the missing sentences in the boxes.**

A man and a woman went to the restaurant – the best restaurant in town, in fact. [3] The man and his wife ordered some onion soup for a starter. The waiter went into the kitchen. "We haven't got any onion soup," the chef said. "Run over to Johnny's restaurant and get me some of their onion soup," the chef said to the waitress.
Johnny's restaurant hadn't got any onion soup so the waitress brought back two bowls of tomato soup. [2]
The man ordered beef, chips and carrots for his main course. [5] Back in the kitchen it was the same problem – no beef and no lamb. The waitress ran to Johnny's and brought back two plates* of chicken. The man and woman were a bit angry. [4] But they tasted* the chicken and they were happy again. It was excellent.
For dessert the man and woman ordered chocolate ice cream. And guess what? No chocolate ice cream in the kitchen. [6]
The man and the woman loved the ice cream. "This restaurant is a bit strange but the food is great," said the man. "I think it really is the best restaurant in town."
"I'm not so sure," said his wife. "I think the best restaurant in town might be Johnny's."
[1] The woman pointed to his ice cream. There was a little flag on the top. It said 'Johnny's restaurant.'

1 "Why do you think that?" asked her husband.
2 The man and woman were surprised but they enjoyed the soup anyway.
3 The waiter took their coats and showed them to a table next to a window.
4 They wanted beef and lamb.
5 His wife ordered lamb, potatoes and cabbage.
6 The waitress went back to Johnny's again.

Vocabulary:
*plate – Teller / taste – kosten, schmecken

★ **11** **Look at the pictures. Write the story *The worst restaurant in town* in your exercise book. Use the words in the box to help you.**

went
dirty
waiter
knife
fly
cola
left
tasted

▶ SB p. 69

Grammar *some / any*

■ **12 Match the questions and answers.**

1 Would you like some orange juice?	☐ No, but I'm going to buy some at the supermarket.
2 Do you want some chocolate?	☐ Yes. Have you got any aspirin?
3 Can you give me some money?	☐ Yes. Two sons and a daughter.
4 Have you got any children?	☐ Yes please, I'm very thirsty.
5 Does your head hurt?	☐ I'm sorry. I haven't got any.
6 Is there any ice cream in the freezer?	☐ No thanks. I don't like sweets.

★ **13 Look in the fridge for thirty seconds and remember as much as you can. Then cover the picture and write sentences.**

1 pears
There are some pears.

2 strawberries
There aren't any strawberries.

3 onions
....

4 grapes
....

5 peppers
....

6 tomatoes
....

7 cabbage
....

8 lamb
....

9 chicken
....

10 chocolate
....

11 cheesecake
....

12 cheese
....

■ **14 Complete the dialogue with *some* or *any*.**

Dad Have [1]......some...... fruit for dessert.
Jenny I don't want [2]......any...... fruit. Haven't we got [3]......some...... ice cream?
Dad Yes, there's [4]......some...... ice cream in the freezer but …
Jenny Well, can I have [5]......some...... ?
Dad No, you can't. You can have [6]......some...... fruit.
Jenny But I don't like fruit.
Dad Don't be silly. Here, have [7]......some...... strawberries.
Jenny Can I have [8]......some...... strawberry ice cream?
Dad No!

▶ SB p. 71

Word File

Food and drink

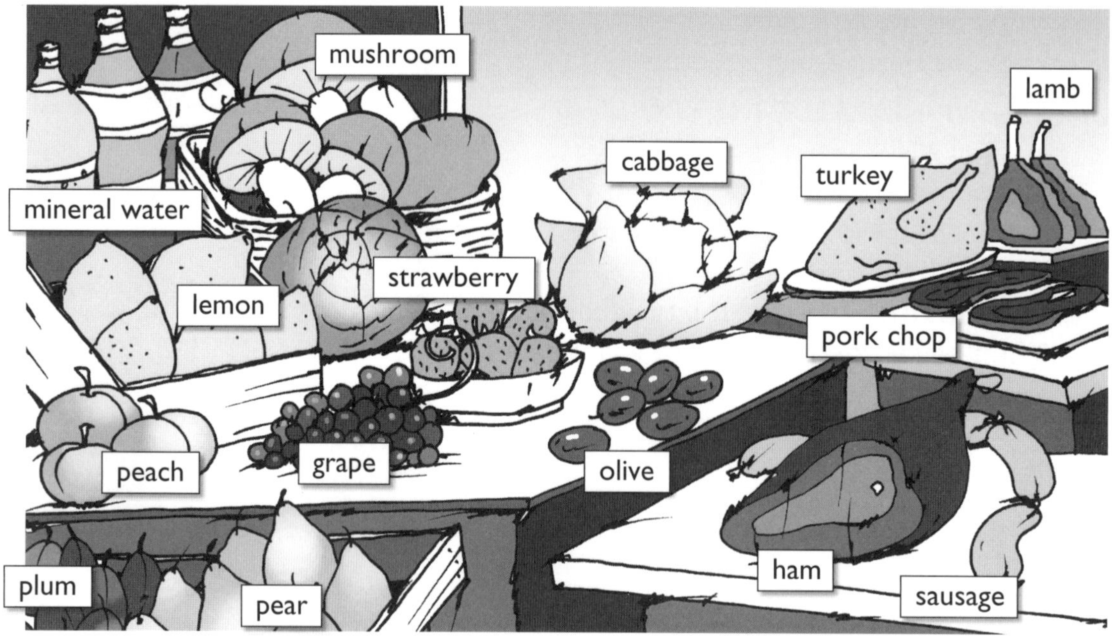

In a restaurant

MORE Words and Phrases

3	slice	*Two big slices of pizza for me, please!*	Stück
	pancake	*I love making pancakes.*	Palatschinke
	pie	*Chicken pie is my favourite meal.*	Pastete, Kuchen
	basket	*There are tomatoes in the shopping basket.*	Korb
5	straightaway	*You're hungry? I'll bring it straightaway!*	sofort
7	**bowl**	*Get two bowls of tomato soup.*	Schüssel
10	cellar	*The top of a salt cellar was on the pizza.*	Streuer
DVD	**by the way**	*By the way, I'm Emma.*	übrigens
	It's no trouble at all		Es ist überhaupt kein Problem

Show what you know Units 6–10

What I CAN DO in English

This page helps you to find out how well you are doing.
Read the statements and draw symbols.

☺ = I'm good at this   ✓ = I can do this with help   ☹ = I need to practise this more

Note:
Wenn du im Buch nachschauen willst, dann helfen dir die Seitenzahlen. Das zeigen sie dir an:

Words

- ◯ I can name at least 5 phrases to tell someone the way, e.g. *turn right ...* . (6/42)
- ◯ I can name at least 14 geographical features, e.g. *mountain*. (7/48)
- ◯ I can name at least 6 activities you can do in your free time, e.g. *watch a DVD*. (8/54)
- ◯ I can name at least 15 food words. (10/66)

Speaking

- ◯ I can ask the way and give instructions for finding the way. (6/43-44)
- ◯ I can make suggestions on what to do, e.g. *Let's build a tree house*. (7/49)
- ◯ I can talk about plans for the weekend. (8/55)
- ◯ I can say what might happen. e.g. *The dog might bite you*. (8/58)
- ◯ I can tell a simple story in the past. (9/63)
- ◯ I can order food and drink in a restaurant. (10/66)

Reading and listening

- ◯ I can listen to and understand instructions in a story (*Gretta and Florestan*). (6/42)
- ◯ I can read and understand dialogues when people ask for the way. (6/43)
- ◯ I can read and understand the story *Looking for Danielle*. (6/45)
- ◯ I can understand the words to the song *Looking for Liz* and sing along. (6/46)
- ◯ I can read and understand the story *Treasure hunt*. (7/50-51)
- ◯ I can listen to, read and understand the sketch *On strike*. (8/56)
- ◯ I can read and understand the story *William the Worrier*. (8/57)
- ◯ I can listen to and understand a story and put pictures in the correct order. (9/60)
- ◯ I can read and understand the story *A new home*. (9/61)
- ◯ I can listen to, read and understand a dialogue in a restaurant. (10/67)
- ◯ I can understand the words to the song *A slice of pizza* and sing along. (10/70)

Writing for my Portfolio

- ◯ I have written an email to a friend with descriptions on how to get to my house. (6/47)
- ◯ I have written a letter home from an imaginary youth camp. (7/53)
- ◯ I have written an invitation to a party. (8/59)
- ◯ I have written an ending to a story. (9/63)
- ◯ I have written a text about a visit to a restaurant. (10/70)

UNIT 11 The curse of the pharaoh

Revision

● 1 **Write the words in the correct place.**

pork
strawberry
onions
green pepper
cabbage
grapes
apple
olives
pumpkin
lemon
potato
beef
lamb
pear
turkey
carrot
chicken
tomato
banana

fruit	vegetables	meat
....	....	....
....	....	....
....	....	....
....	....	....
....	....	....
....	....	
	....	
	....	

■ 2 **Write *some* or *any*.**

Tim So what do you need for dinner tonight, Aylin?

Aylin Hmmm, let me see, I've got [1]...................... lamb, and I've got [2]...................... onions, but we haven't got [3]...................... green peppers.

Tim OK, so I get [4]...................... peppers?

Aylin Wait a minute. Let me see … what else do I need? [5]...................... black olives maybe. And another question: are there [6]...................... potatoes left?

Tim No, I don't think so.

Aylin OK, get [7]...................... potatoes, too. And [8]...................... tomatoes. And I don't think there are [9]...................... grapes for the fruit salad. Get [10]...................... grapes, mum loves them.

Tim OK.

● 3 **Write the verbs in brackets in the past simple.**

Yesterday we [1].................................. (go) to a very nice restaurant. Aunt Maria [2].................................. (invite) us because it was her birthday. I [3].................................. (eat) so much that I [4].................................. (find) it difficult to get up from the table after dinner. At home I [5].................................. (feel) a bit sick. I [6].................................. (tell) mum and she [7].................................. (give) me something to drink. That really [8].................................. (help) me. Then I just [9].................................. (fall) into my bed and [10].................................. (sleep) for more than ten hours.

END OF REVISION SECTION

■ **4** **Do the puzzle and find the secret word.**

1								L		
2	R							N		
3										
4						Y				
5								B		
6										
7				H					H	
8						X				

1 

2 They had lots of gods in ancient Egypt – … was very important.

3 

4 People in ancient Egypt wrote on pieces of … .

5 

6 The … Nile was very important.

7 A king in ancient Egypt was called a … .

8 The … has a human's head and a lion's body.

The secret word is ....

■ **5** **Match to make sentences.**

1 We know about life in ancient Egypt
2 People in ancient Egypt wore light clothes
3 People wore sandals or
4 The sandals were made
5 Men and women cared about their looks and
6 Many Egyptians worked as farmers but
7 Weavers made beautiful clothes and people
8 People ate fish, meat, fruit
9 Hunting and fishing were the most
10 Children played ball games

☐ went barefoot.
☐ they also had to help build the pyramids.
☐ paid for them with salt, food and other things.
☐ from objects found in tombs.
☐ and a lot of vegetables.
☐ because it was very hot.
☐ popular sports for the men.
☐ wore make-up and jewellery.
☐ and had little animals made from wood.
☐ of palm leaves.

▶ SB p. 77

6 Put the dialogue in the correct order.

> **Vocabulary:**
> *How long did they take? – Wie lange brauchten sie?

- [ ] **A** How long did they take?*
- [ ] **A** That's a lot of stones!
- [ ] **A** How heavy?
- [ ] **A** Wow – that's high! How long is it?
- [1] **A** Did you go to a pyramid when you were in Egypt?
- [ ] **B** More than 230 metres. And they needed a hundred thousand men to build it.
- [ ] **B** About twenty years. And it was really hard work. The stones were heavy.
- [ ] **B** Well, each one was about two thousand kilograms! And ... the pyramid's got over two million stones in it.
- [ ] **B** Yes, we went to the one for Pharaoh Khufu. It was amazing! You know, it's over 140 metres high.

7 Put the verbs in the box in the correct places.

believed
broke
climbed
died
found
guarded
knew
put
stole
woke

When a pharaoh [1]................................., the priests [2]................................. the mummy inside a pyramid. The ancient Egyptians [3]................................. that, after a long time, the pharaoh's spirit [4]................................. up and [5]................................. up the steps of the pyramid to meet Ra, the sun god. The people put things like food, clothes and jewellery in the pyramid with the mummy.

Of course, everyone [6]................................. that there were wonderful things inside the pyramid, so soldiers [7]................................. the tombs day and night to stop thieves. But hundreds of years later, robbers [8]................................. into the pyramids. They [9]................................. the tombs and [10]................................. the clothes and jewellery.

8 Match.

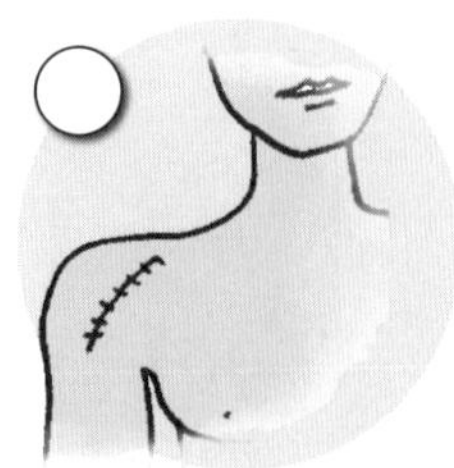

1 a canary
2 servants
3 a telegram
4 a candle
5 treasure
6 cheek
7 bandages
8 a wound

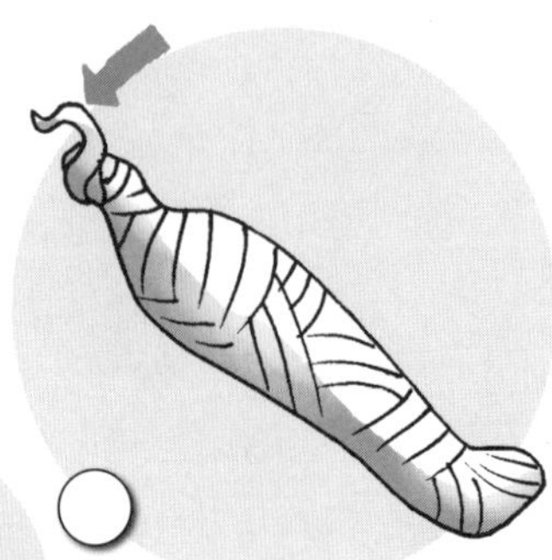

▶ SB p. 79

■ **9** **How much can you remember? Complete the text with one word in each space. Then check in the Student's Book on page 78.**

One of the most [1]f...amous... Pharaohs was Tutankhamun. He became Pharaoh when he was [2]n...ine... , but he died when he was only [3]n...ineteen... . He is famous because the [4]r...obbers... did not find his tomb. When an [5]E...nglish man... called Howard [6]C...arter... found the tomb of Tutankhamun in 1922, it was still full of wonderful [7]c...lothes... and [8]j...ewellery... .

■ **10** **Read the summary. There is a mistake in each sentence. Write the correct word.**

The curse of the pharaoh

1 Hannah, Luke and their parents went to visit a pyramid with a ~~friend~~. ...guide...

2 The guide told them about ~~a group of tourists~~ who tried to find a tomb in the pyramid, but never came back. ...Some scientists...

3 He said: "The ~~story~~ of the pharaoh killed them!" ...curse...

4 Hannah laughed and ~~shouted~~ something to Luke, but Luke didn't hear her. ...whispered...

5 "Look!" ~~he~~ said. "There's a hole in the ~~floor~~!" ...wall...

6 They climbed through the hole, and suddenly there was a loud wind, and a stone closed the hole. ...noise...

7 The children tried to break the stone but they couldn't – they couldn't get out again. ...move...

8 So they walked along a corridor in the dark until they saw a window. They opened it and looked out. ....

9 They saw men building another pyramid. The men talked like people from ancient Egypt! ....

★ **11** **Write the story. Make up your own ending.**

The pharaoh died and the people were very unhappy. So they buried him in a gigantic pyramid, where he was very safe. This is because the inside of the pyramid is like a labyrinth. The slaves carried the pharaoh into a chamber and pushed a big stone infront of the entrance. 3,000 years later 2 men were searching for the chamber. After a while they found it.

▶ SB p. 80

Grammar Irregular plurals

■ **12** **Write one word in each box.**

Singular	Plural
man	men
woman	
	children
person	
foot	

Singular	Plural
	teeth
fish	
knife	
	thieves
sheep	

■ **13** **Use words from 12 to complete the conversations.**

1 **A** Are there any forks in the drawer?
B Er – no, only spoons* and ....

2 **A** Can I wear your shoes?
B Don't be silly – my .... are smaller than yours.

3 **A** Did you catch anything in the river today?
B Yes, we caught ten really nice ....

4 **A** My older sister is twenty-two and she has a husband.
B Has she got any .... ?

5 **A** I can't go to sleep!
B Why don't you count .... ?

Vocabulary: *spoon – Löffel

● **14** **Match the questions and pictures.**

1 Who found the mummy?
2 Who wrote this email?
3 Who gave him the present?
4 Who went with you to Egypt?
5 Who broke the vase?

■ **15** **Write the questions.**

1 Someone phoned me last night!
Who ....phoned you.......... ?

2 Someone gave Sally a present yesterday.
Who .... ?

3 Someone ate all the chocolate!
Who .... ?

4 There are six girls in the class – one of them loves Billy!
Who .... ?

5 I've got a lot of friends – one of them lives in that house.
Who .... ?

▶ SB p. 81

Word File

In ancient Egypt

On a farm

Jobs

MORE Words and Phrases

2	goose (pl geese)	*The farmer has lots of geese on his farm.*	Gans
	human		Mensch; menschlich
	invent	*Alexander Bell invented the telephone.*	erfinden
	per cent (%)	*90 per cent of Egyptians live near the Nile.*	Prozent (%)
	tricky	*This question is tricky because there are actually two correct answers.*	betrügerisch; hier: schwierig, kompliziert
	actually		eigentlich; hier: tatsächlich
	bath	*When it is hot I have a bath every day.*	Bad
	plant	*Because of the River Nile, plants grow well in Egypt.*	Pflanze
	religion	*Buddhism and Islam are important religions in Asia.*	Religion
	cross		Kreuz
	mostly	*They had the head of humans, mostly kings.*	meistens
	probably	*Eye glasses probably came from Italy.*	vermutlich
3	care about …	*Egyptians cared a lot about their looks.*	sich aus … etwas machen
	made of	*The sandals were made of palm leaves.*	aus … gemacht
	pay (for)	*People paid for the clothes with food and other things.*	bezahlen
	fat	*The Egyptians used the horn and the fat of the animals.*	Fett
	light	*Wear something light today. It's very hot.*	leicht
	worker	*Many workers helped to build the pyramids.*	Arbeiter/in
	looks	*Looks were very important to the Ancient Egyptians.*	Blick, Aussehen
	sell	*They sell a lot of different perfumes at the chemist's.*	verkaufen
	melt		schmelzen
	smell		riechen
5	**leaf** (pl leaves)	*The leaves of palm trees are huge.*	Blatt
7	**indeed**	*Yes, it was indeed.*	tatsächlich
8	spirit	*The pharaoh was dead, but people believed his spirit lived on.*	Geist
	step	*You must climb up the steps to get a good view.*	Stufe
	guard	*The 'curse of the pharaohs' helped guard the treasure.*	Wache
	Englishman	*An Englishman found Tutankhamun's tomb.*	Engländer
	full of	*The pyramid was full of wonderful clothes and jewellery.*	voll von
	steal	*Robbers stole everything inside the pyramids.*	stehlen
9	jam		Marmelade
	choose	*Did you choose strawberry or apricot jam?*	auswählen
10	born	*He was born in England.*	geboren sein/werden
	discover	*He discovered the tomb.*	entdecken
	few	*A few days later, an insect bit Carter on the cheek.*	einige, wenig
	cheek		Backe
	wound	*There was the same wound on the pharaoh's cheek.*	Wunde
12	**centre (BE)**	*The shops are all in the city centre.*	Zentrum, Mitte
	group	*I went on holiday with a group of friends last year.*	Gruppe
	torch	*To explore tombs, you must use a torch.*	Taschenlampe
	second	*Wait a second! I forgot my bag.*	Sekunde
	fill	*Fill the pot with water.*	füllen
	out loud	*Hannah laughed out loud.*	laut
14	**fall over**	*The little girl fell over and cut her knee.*	hinfallen; umfallen
	wide		weit
	voice	*Suddenly they heard voices.*	Stimme
G	**tooth** (pl teeth)	*You have nice teeth.*	Zahn

UNIT 12 Families

Revision

1 Match to make sentences.

1 An Egyptian king was called a
2 When a pharaoh died, the people put him
3 The Nile is still a very important
4 It took twenty years to build a
5 The sphinx was
6 Papyrus was

☐ in a tomb.
☐ half human, half lion.
☐ pharaoh.
☐ river in Egypt.
☐ a kind of paper.
☐ pyramid.

2 Complete. Write one word each time.

1 There are two .... and six .... in the picture.

2 There are two .... and five .... in the picture.

3 In the picture there are two .... and four ....

4 These two .... have got perfect .... !

3 Write the words in the correct order to make questions.

1 tombs / Who / the / guarded / ?
Who guarded the tombs?
2 tomb / found / Who / Tutankhamun's / ?
....
3 the / put / mummies / Who / in / pyramids / the / ?
....
4 when / Who / was / he / 19 / died / ?
....
5 visited / with / pyramid / Who / a / sister / his / ?
....
6 in / discovered / Who / a / the / hole / wall / ?
....

END OF REVISION SECTION

■ **4** **Find the fourteen family words. Look in all directions.**

N	E	R	D	L	I	H	C	D	N	A	R	G
N	S	E	A	I	R	E	T	H	G	U	A	D
I	T	H	R	U	J	N	A	S	O	B	E	S
S	E	T	L	A	N	D	M	T	I	R	I	O
U	L	A	R	E	H	T	O	M	Q	S	K	N
O	P	F	R	A	W	B	R	O	T	H	E	R
C	I	Y	L	I	M	A	F	E	Y	I	W	N
G	R	A	N	D	P	A	R	E	N	T	S	A
W	T	S	X	E	L	C	N	U	H	S	A	T

....
....
....
....
....
....
....
....
....
....
....
....
....
....

■ **5** **Put the text in the correct order.**

☐ are the world's largest family. Mr and
☐ birth, she had twins or triplets. So now
☐ in the same small town, and eighteen
☐ many grandchildren they've got! They still live
☐ Mrs Albina got married when they were very
☐ of their children still live with them.
1 The Albina family live in Chile, and they
☐ they've got 53 children, but they don't know how
☐ young, and every time that Mrs Albina gave

★ **6** **Work out how old the following people are.**

Mr King is nine times as old as* his granddaughter Hanna.
His son John is three years older than his daughter Susan.
Susan is half as old as Mrs King.
Together John's children, the twins, are as old as their aunt Susan.
Susan's daughter Hanna is 8. She's half as old as the twins.

Mr King: .... Mrs King: ....
John King: .... Susan King: ....
The twins: .... Hanna: ....8....

Vocabulary: *nine times as old as – neun Mal so alt wie …

▶ SB p. 82

7 What do they like? Write sentences.

1 Ron likes playing basketball.
2 ....
3 ....
4 ....
5 ....
6 ....

8 Look at page 83 of the Student's Book. Match to make sentences about the Boehmer family.

1 Everyone in the Boehmer	☐ 1989 and soon all the children were in the show.
2 Even their dog Bosco	☐ hours every week but they also do other things.
3 They started their first shows in	☐ family is a juggler.
4 They practise for eight to ten	☐ doing the shows.
5 One son likes working out, and one	☐ is part of the show.
6 They all love learning new tricks and	☐ of the daughters likes water skiing and running.

9 Read the text on page 84 of the Student's Book again, and then write who said what in an interview. Write *Lisa*, *Amar*, *Denise* or *Les*.

1 My real dad moved out five years ago. Lisa
2 I live in a large flat. ....
3 My cousin lived with us for two years. ....
4 We live in a nice house outside the city centre. ....
5 We had to come here eight years ago. ....
6 The school is right here in the camp. ....
7 I don't see my dad very often. ....
8 My grandparents don't live far away from us. ....

SB p. 84

Grammar *like(s) doing*

■ 10 **Write sentences about the people below.**

Example:
Christopher likes dancing, but he doesn't like singing.

1 Ada ....

2 Joe ....

3 Harry ....

4 Tanya ....

5 My grandpa ....

■ 11 **Complete the text from the *Wonderman files*.**

When I was a kid, I liked all kinds of sports. I liked [1] ....  , I liked [2] .... , and I even liked [3] .... . Today I'm a bit lazy. I don't like [4] ....  in the morning, I don't like [5] ....  or [6] .... . What do I like? I like [7] ....  television, [8] ....  and [9] ....  !!

Grammar *must/mustn't*

Vocabulary: *boots – Stiefel

● 12 **Write *must* or *mustn't*.**

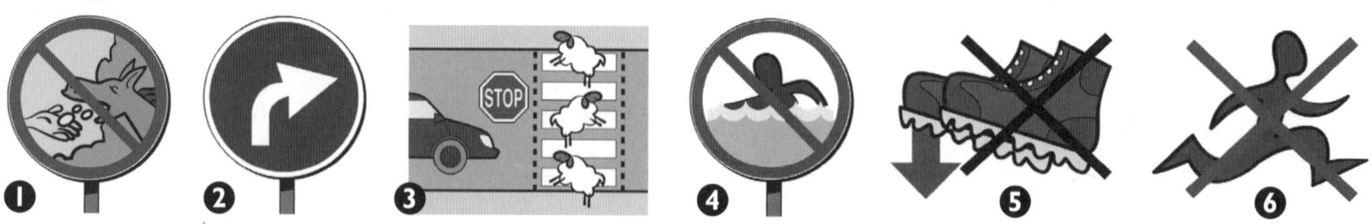

1 You mustn't feed the animals.
2 You must turn right at the crossing.
3 You must stop for sheep crossing.
4 You mustn't swim here.
5 You mustn't leave your boots* here.
6 You mustn't run in the corridors.

▶ SB p. 87

13 Complete the dialogue with the sentences in the box.

Is there anything I can do?
~~Midnight as usual.~~
or you'll feel bad all night.
You must be home by midnight.

Jo OK Mum, I'm off to the youth club.

Mum Wait, Jo. [1] You must be home by midnight

Jo I know, Mum. [2] Midnight

Mum And you mustn't eat and drink too much, [3] as you'll feel bad all night

Jo I know, Mum. I never eat too much.

Mum But you drink too much cola, I know you. You mustn't, OK?

Jo OK. [4] Is there anything I can do?

Mum Sure. You must have fun.

Jo Ha, ha. Is that an order?

★ 14 My aunty Mary doesn't like children. Write down the things you *mustn't* do in her house. Use the words in the box to help you.

run
use
listen
take
put
downstairs

1 You mustn't put shoes on the bed!
2 You mustn't listen to music in the bed!
3 You mustn't take out food of the fridge!
4 You mustn't run downstairs!
5 You mustn't use the telephone!

▶ SB p. 87

Word File In a family

MORE Words and Phrases

3	**possible**	*Juggling is possible for almost everyone.*	möglich
	give birth to	*She gave birth to twins.*	zur Welt bringen
4	**practise**	*I practise every day.*	üben
	eldest	*She is the eldest daughter.*	älteste, r, s
	work out	*If you work out a lot you will get strong.*	trainieren
	roller-skate	*It's fun to roller-skate!*	Skaten
	anybody	*Anybody can juggle.*	jeder; ein jeder
	daughter	*The eldest daughter likes water skiing.*	Tochter
7	**university**	*There is no university in this town.*	Universität
	refugee camp		Flüchtlingslager
	Portuguese	*My friend Rui speaks Portuguese.*	Portugiese/in; portugiesisch
	because (of)		weil, auf Grund von
	war	*We had to leave because of the war.*	Krieg
	study	*My cousin studied at the university in Birmingham.*	studieren
	translate	*My uncle translates from Portuguese into English.*	übersetzen
8	the dishes (pl)	*Can you do the dishes?*	das Geschirr (spülen)
	till	*Can I stay out till ten o'clock?*	bis
9	**borrow** (from)	*Can I borrow a ring from you?*	ausleihen (von)
	print out	*I don't print out web pages.*	ausdrucken
	delete	*Oops, I have deleted your file.*	streichen, löschen
	chat	*Don't chat with strangers.*	plaudern, chatten
	Forget it!		Vergiss es!
	switch off/on	*Switch off the computer!*	aus/einschalten
12	mathematician		Mathematiker/in
	genius	*He was a mathematician and a genius.*	Genie
	visitor	*They don't like visitors.*	Besucher

UNIT 13 Magic

Revision

■ **1 Complete the dialogue with the sentences in the box.**

> That's my cousin Fred.
>
> Is that your grandpa?
>
> Are you sure it's Fred?
>
> Was all your family there?
>
> Yes, he's my father's brother.

Nina Can I have a look at the photos, Jane?
Jane Yes, sure. Here you are.
Nina They're lovely. 1 ....
Jane Yes, that's my grandfather. It was his birthday.
Nina There's a lot of people in the picture. 2 ....
Jane Yes, even my uncle from Australia.
Nina Oh, you've got an uncle in Australia?
Jane 3 .... He went there twenty years ago.
Nina And who's that?
Jane 4 .... He's Aunt Jenny's son. Do you remember her?
Nina Of course I do. I also remember Fred, but this guy looks really cool. 5 ....
Jane (*laughs*) Of course, I am. And you're right. He looks pretty good now.

■ **2 Complete another text from the *Wonderman files*. Use *-ing* forms.**

When I was a kid I liked 1 .... 

to school.

I liked 2 ....  , I liked 3 .... 

French, and I liked 4 ....  pictures a lot.

These days I'm a bit lazy. I don't like 5 ....  , and I don't like

6 ....  to concerts. I like 7 ....  TV,

I like 8 ....  computer games and most of all …
I like doing nothing. 

● **3 Complete with *must* or *mustn't*.**

Mum:
When Uncle Fred comes to visit …
you 1 .... help him with his bags,
you 2 .... be nice to him,
you 3 .... play loud music,
you 4 .... watch TV all the time
and you 5 .... talk to him.
And please don't forget:
you 6 .... say "Thank you"
when he gives you a present!

END OF REVISION SECTION

● **4** **Read the sentences and write the names of the ghosts under the correct pictures.**

....

1 Bobby is floating above the floor.
2 Stacey is walking through a door.
3 Larry is making a blood stain.
4 Poppy is screaming.
5 Jimmy is rattling his rusty chains.

■ **5** **Read the sketch and complete with the words in the box.**

School for Ghosts II

through	chains
done	carefully
push	easily
screaming	take

Teacher OK, so who can [1].................................. their head off?

Teenage ghost 1 I can.

Teacher Good. Show us then. But do it [2].. .

Teenage ghost 1 OK, first I take it between my hands, then turn it to the right, then to the left, and then – take it off!

Teacher Very good! You did really well. You see, his head came off [3].................................. . Who wants to go next?

Teenage ghosts Me! Me! Me! Me!

Teacher OK, OK. Stop [4].................................. . One at a time. OK, Thomas. You're next.

Teenage ghost 2 So I take it between my hands, then turn it to the right then to the left, and then – take it off!

Teacher Good! That went well, too. OK, Jenny. It's your turn.

(10 minutes later.)

Teacher Good. That was really fast. Well [5].................................. everyone. Now let's put them back on again.

Teenage ghost 1 Hey, watch out. Don't [6].................................. me.

Teenage ghost 2 You pushed me!!

Teacher Stop it, stop it!

Teenage ghost 1 Hey, where's my head?

Teenage ghost 2 Careful. Oh no. Where's my head?

Teacher Come on, stop fighting. Pick up your heads. Bedtime. No rattling of [7].................................. tonight! Walk straight [8].................................. the walls to bed.

Teenage ghost 2 Sir? Sir? This is not my head! Can you help me, please?

Teacher Ohhhh! Teenagers!

▶ SB p. 89

6 Write the numbers of the sentences in the pictures.

1 I can pass through a locked door easily.
2 Gozo likes screaming loudly.
3 Now you have to walk quietly.
4 Don't go so fast!
5 A ghost must walk through a wall very slowly.
6 She can take off her head really well.

7 Write the phrases under the pictures.

Vocabulary:
*lose – verlieren

the neighbour's garden	put out a fire	fill a pot with water
pick up a ball	a lot of smoke	a car behind the house
climb over a fence	shout	a car in front of the house
look through the bushes	look for the ball	lose* a shoe

1

2

3

4

5

6

7

8

9

10
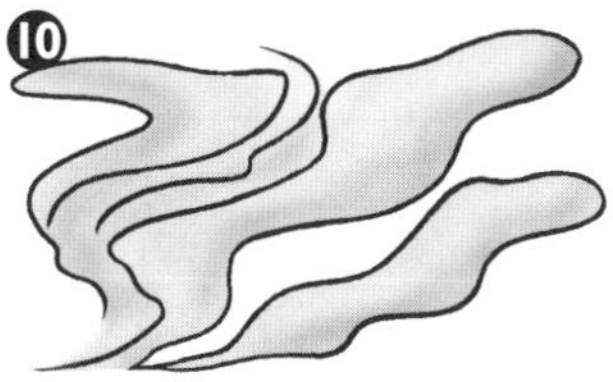

11

12

SB p. 90

★ **8** **Read the summary of *Abracadabra, one, two, three* and write one word each time to complete it.**

Vocabulary:
*complain – sich beschweren
liquid – Flüssigkeit

Debbie and her brother Robert were playing football behind the house. The ball landed in the garden next door. Robert climbed over the 1 .... 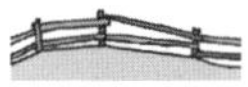 to get it. The ball was next to the 2 ....  of their neighbour, Mr Blogg. He didn't like the children and Robert was a bit scared. Mr Blogg saw Robert and shouted. Robert jumped back over the fence. Mr Blogg threw their ball back. But now it had a big 3 .... 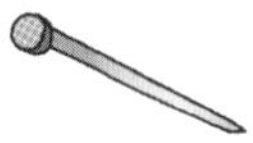 in it.

The next Saturday was Debbie's birthday. She had a party in the garden with lots of friends. They made a fire in the garden and made 4 .... 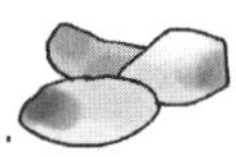 on it. Mr Blogg complained* about the smoke and the noise. Three days later, their cat Snowy was ill. Debbie was sure Mr Blogg had something to do with it.

Debbie had a book on magic. It had lots of 5 ....  in it. She wanted to put a spell on Mr Blogg. They needed five things from Mr Blogg to make the spell. That night, the children climbed into his garden. They found five things: half a cigar, a piece of bread, an old sock, half a hot dog and a 6 ....  .

The next morning they put all the things in a pot and filled it with water. They put the pot on the 7 ....  and made a brown liquid*.

Then they went back to Mr Blogg's garden and  8 .... the brown liquid on the grass. Suddenly Mr Blogg arrived and shouted at them, and the children ran away quickly.

The children spent the afternoon at their grandmother's house. When they got back home, there was a police car outside the house.

'What's the matter?' Robert asked the policeman.

'Mr Blogg had a car accident in town,' the policeman told them. 'And when we looked in his 9 ....  we found a lot of stolen computers. Your neighbour's in 10 ....  now.' The children smiled. What a great spell!

★ **9** **Complete the sentences about the story.**

1 Debbie and Robert lived next ....
2 Mr Blogg didn't like ....
3 He did lots of terrible things – for example, he put a nail ....
4 The children made ....
5 They needed five ....
6 They sprinkled ....
7 Mr Blogg had a car accident and the police found ....
8 The spell worked because ....

★ **10** **Write a story called *The wrong spell.* Think about your answers to these questions to help you write the story.**

1 Who made the spell? ....
2 What was the spell for? ....
3 How did he or she make the spell? ....
4 Why did it go wrong? ....
5 What happened? ....

▶ SB p. 92

Grammar Adverbs of manner

11 Use the adverbs of the adjectives in brackets to complete the sentences.

1 **A** He plays football really .... (good)
B Yes, he wants to be a star.

2 **A** I don't think the teacher was very happy.
B No, she looked at us really .... (angry)

3 **A** Sh! Talk .... (quiet)
B Why?
A Henry's trying to sleep.

4 **A** Are we in a hurry?
B No.
A So, don't walk so .... (quick)

5 **A** Slower, Dad, slower!
B Yes, you're driving too .... (fast)

6 **A** Is the climb very difficult?
B Yes, so you should go very .... (careful)

12 Complete the sentences with the adverbs of the adjectives in the box.

bad
careful
good
happy
fast
slow

1 She's running very ....

2 He's working really ....

3 It's walking .... to the other side of the street.

4 She's laughing ....

5 I did .... in the test today.

6 They're playing very ....

13 Read the text and circle the correct options.

I'm a ghost hunter! I hunt ghosts and when I catch them I take them to a castle on an island in the north of Scotland. There they can rattle their chains and make *loud / loudly* noises. There they can wait *quiet / quietly* for other ghosts. They can go 'Boo!' and laugh *happy / happily* when the other ghosts are scared. On the island they can't scare people like you and me.
I'm not scared *easy / easily*. A good ghost hunter isn't scared of ghosts! But sometimes ghosts make me *nervous / nervously*, because they play tricks. They hide their heads, and they go through walls *quick / quickly*. And when I follow them, I hit my head. Hunting ghosts is what I do *good / well*. Only I sometimes have bad dreams. I dream that a big ghost catches me and takes me to the north of Scotland. There, hundreds of *angry / angrily* ghosts are waiting for me. Luckily it's only a dream.

▶ SB p. 93

Word File At home

MORE Words and Phrases

1	**pass through**	*They say ghosts can pass through walls.*	durchgehen
	float	*Ghosts float above the ground.*	hier: schweben
	rattle		klappern, rasseln
	chain	*The ghosts rattled their chains.*	Kette
	nasty		scheußlich, grässlich, widerlich
	scream	*Some people scream when they're frightened.*	schreien; kreischen
2	**teach**	*She wants to teach them French.*	unterrichten
	lock	*Lock the door, John!*	abschließen
	get stuck	*If you get stuck, I'll pull you out.*	festsitzen, steckenbleiben
5	nail	*The picture was hanging on a nail.*	Nagel
	put a spell on	*Shall we put a spell on that man?*	verzaubern
	feather	*The bird had blue and red feathers.*	Feder
	sprinkle	*Can you sprinkle some salt on the carrots?*	streuen, besprengen, sprühen
	(car) boot	*The boot of this car is too small.*	Kofferraum
	prison	*People who steal things get put in prison.*	Gefängnis
	someone	*Can you put a spell on someone?*	irgend jemand
6	unfriendly	*Some people are nice but others are unfriendly.*	unfreundlich
	roast	*Can we roast these potatoes?*	rösten
	rotten	*Rotten fish smells very bad.*	verfault, verdorben
	magic	*I don't believe in magic – do you?*	Magie, Zauber
	beer	*She doesn't drink beer.*	Bier
	pot		Topf
	stuff	*What's that stuff? I don't know!*	Zeug
	police officer	*The police officer left the room.*	Polizeibeamter
	doorbell	*After ten minutes they heard the doorbell.*	Türglocke
	glad	*Debbie was glad Mr Blogg wasn't in hospital.*	froh
	put out	*Dad told them to put out the fire.*	löschen
	scared of	*Robert was scared of Mr Blogg.*	Angst haben
	trainers	*He lost one of his trainers.*	Turnschuhe
8	**beat**	*They beat the other team.*	schlagen, besiegen
	definitely	*Oh yeah, definitely!*	eindeutig, definitiv, auf jeden Fall
	good-looking	*The sisters are cool and good-looking.*	gutaussehend
	nineties	*It's from the nineties, but still a great TV series.*	neunziger Jahre
	reason	*There are a lot of reasons why she likes the TV series.*	Grund
	serious	*She's not as serious as the others can be.*	ernst
10	**neck**	*Some ghosts have chains round their necks.*	Hals; Nacken

Revision

● 1 Write the correct opposites using the words in the box.

cold, loud, sad, interesting, slow, difficult

1 happy ....
2 quiet ....
3 easy ....
4 hot ....
5 quick ....
6 boring ....

● 2 Complete with the adverbs of the adjectives in brackets.

Myrtle the ghost

opened the door [1].. (slow). Where were the ghost hunters? She listened [2].. (careful). Everything was quiet. Too quiet? Myrtle floated [3].. (quick) to the other side and looked out of the window. No ghost hunters. She laughed [4].. (happy). Maybe they were scared of her. After all, she was a very scary ghost. "You're doing your job really [5].. (good)." She could hear the words of her father, the great Syltin the Scary, in her head. Suddenly there was a strange sound. Myrtle screamed [6].. (loud). Were the ghost hunters back? No, it was only Tabs her cat. "Stop scaring me!" Myrtle shouted at the cat. Now the cat was scared and ran away very [7].. (fast).

■ 3 Complete with the adverbs of the words in the box.

good, slow, quick, loud, careful, bad, quiet

1 Please talk .... The baby's sleeping!
2 She won because she played very ....
3 When Sue came in with the scary mask on, everyone screamed ....
4 I'm not a good singer – I sing very ....
5 I'm running .... because I'm very, very tired!
6 We were late so we ate lunch .... and left.
7 Drive .... ! It's raining.

END OF REVISION SECTION

▶ SB p. 94

■ **4** **What kind of places do they live in? Write down the types of homes.**

1 **Martin** I like it because it's a home I can drive around in. Motor home
2 **Connie** I live on the 20th floor – and I really like it. Sky scraper
3 **Jim** My house has got a lovely garden and two bedrooms. And it's only got one floor – I like that. bungalow
4 **Arya** We've got a special weekend house. It's in the woods and to get in you have to climb up. treehouse

● **5** **Do the puzzle and find the secret word.**

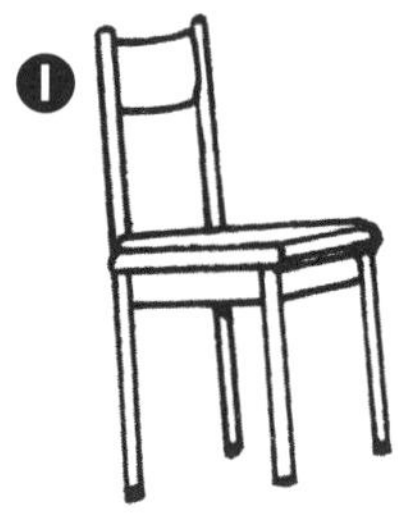
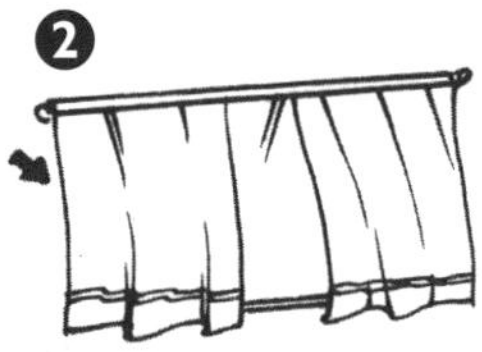
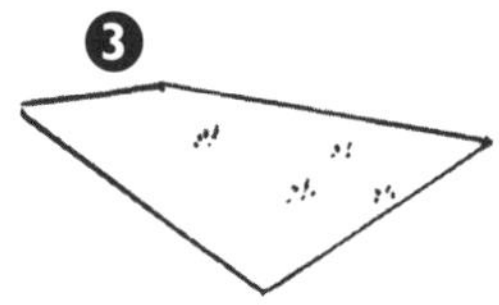

1							C	H	A	I	R		
2						C	U	R	T	A	I	N	S
3				C	A	R	P	E	T				
4	W	A	R	D	R	O	B	E					
5					C	O	O	K	E	R			
6						R	A	D	I	A	T	O	R
7						F	R	I	D	G	E		
8					B	E	D						

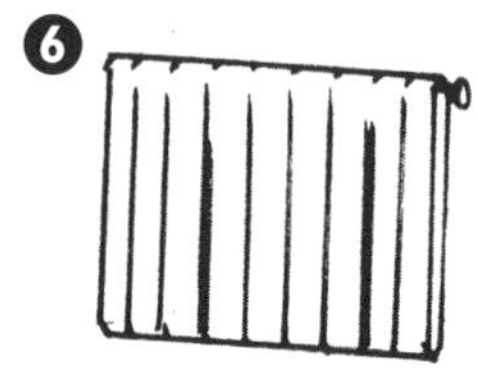
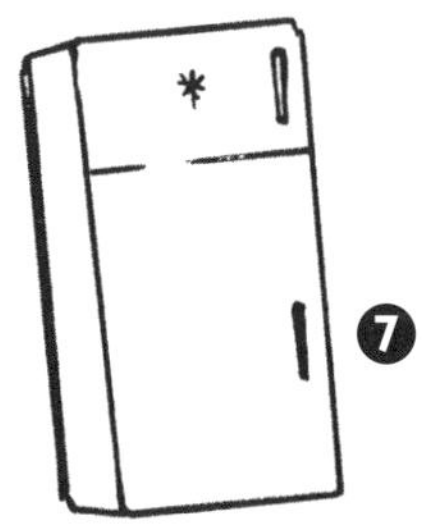

The secret word is cupboard

● **6** **Find fourteen more words for things in a room and write sentences. (↓→)**

B	E	D	P	W	F	T	O	L	G
E	D	P	T	A	B	L	E	E	Z
D	R	X	F	R	I	D	G	E	R
S	Y	R	A	D	I	A	T	O	R
T	X	A	Z	R	H	Y	A	Z	I
A	C	D	S	O	F	A	B	E	D
B	V	I	T	B	E	D	L	R	C
L	B	A	X	E	S	B	E	D	H
E	E	T	Y	T	J	J	O	M	A
T	S	O	F	A	U	I	P	N	I
T	F	R	I	D	G	E	W	Y	R

Example:
There are two fridges.
There's one Wardrobe
There are two sofas
There's one Chair
There are five Beds
There are two radiators
There are three tables

▶ SB p. 95

■ **7** **a Draw these items of furniture* in the room below.**

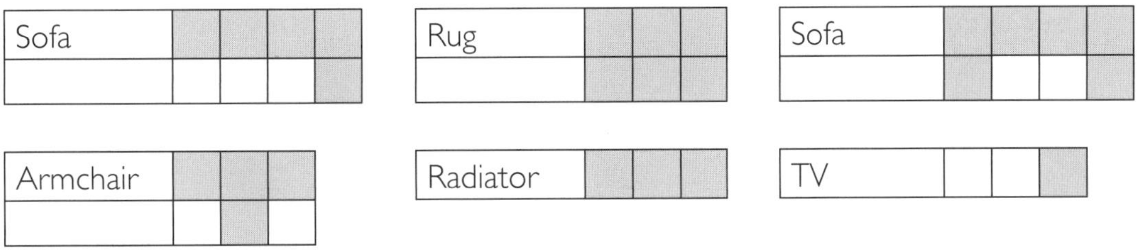

	A	B	C	D	E	F	G	H	I	J	K	L	M	N	O	P	Q	R	S	T	U	V	W	X	Y	Z
1																										
2																										
3																										
4																										
5																										
6																										
7																										
8																										
9																										

b Work with a partner. Take turns to guess where you partner's furniture is. Who finds all the furniture first wins the game.

"Is there anything on B12?" *"Yes, my sofa. Have another guess."*
"No there isn't. It's my turn now."

Vocabulary:
*furniture – Möbel

★ **8** **Choose one of the following people. Write about the favourite room in their house.**

Vocabulary:
*study – Arbeitszimmer

Example:
Natasha Black lives in London. She's a computer expert. Her favourite room is her study. There, she's got a very powerful computer with a large flat screen. She loves working on her computer. She also uses it to write emails to her friends and to make phone calls to her sister in New York.*

....

....

....

....

▶ SB p. 97

Grammar *whose*, possessive *'s*, possessive pronouns

■ **9** **Here are some inventions from the Ideas Office. Which invention was whose idea? Write sentences.**

Example:

Vocabulary: *picker – Pflücker/in

1 *The homework machine was Professor Albu's idea.*
2 ....
3 ....
4 ....
5 ....

★ **10** **Write the questions.**

1 ....?
The automatic vegetable picker* was Professor Newt's idea.
2 ....?
The automatic vegetable cooker was Professor Toad's idea.
3 ....?
The automatic vegetable feeder was my idea.

▶ SB p. 99

★ **11** **Write questions and answers.**

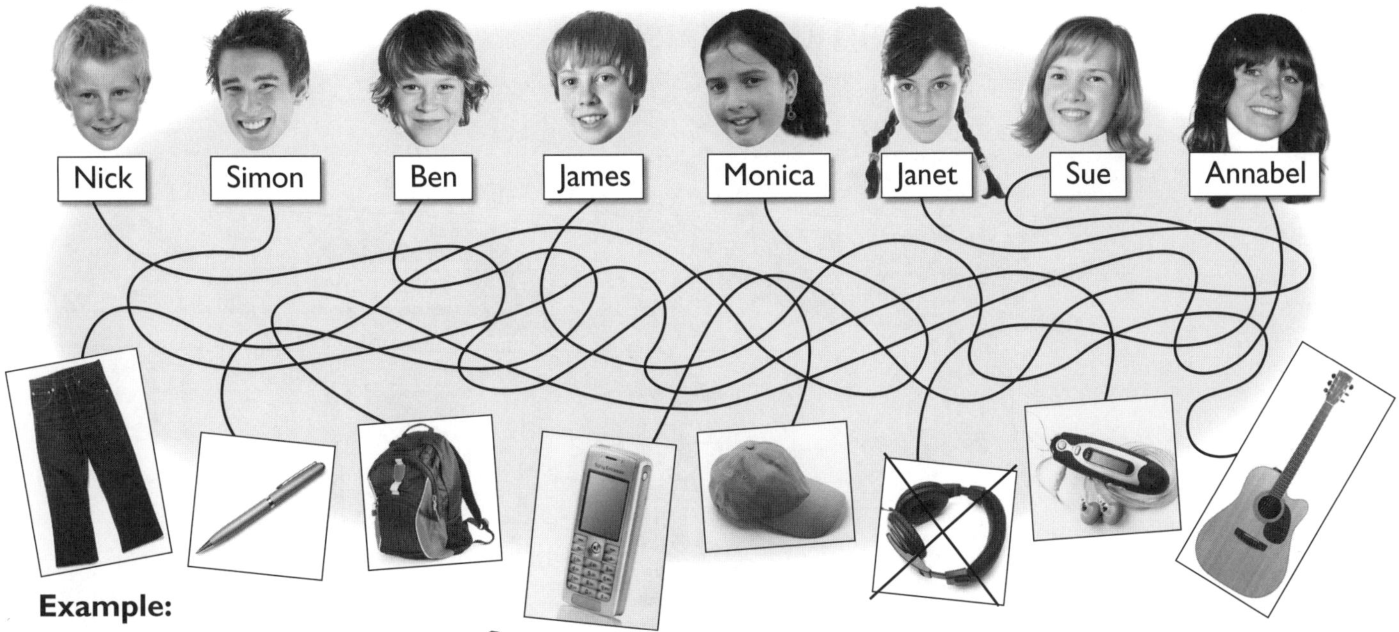

Example:

1 **A** *Whose are those headphones?*
B *They're Sue's.*

2 **A** *Whose are* ....?
B *They're* ....

3 **A** ....?
B ....

4 **A** ....?
B ....

5 **A** ....?
B ....

6 **A** ....?
B ....

7 **A** ....?
B ....

8 **A** ....?
B ....

■ **12** **Complete the dialogue with the possessive pronouns.**

hers
yours
mine

Dimitri I hate this!
Ron Well, whose idea was it to go for a walk?
Dimitri It certainly wasn't [1]....................................... .
Ron No? I thought it was [2]....................................... .
Dimitri Never. Check with Anna, I think it was [3]....................................... .
Ron I can't, she's too far ahead already.

■ **13** **Complete with the possessive pronouns in the box.**

mine
theirs
ours
his
mine
theirs

Camp guide Fred and Hannah, is this your GPS?
Fred and Hannah Yes, it's [1]....................................... .
Camp guide And is this your cap, Tony?
Tony No, it isn't [2]....................................... . Ask Peter. I think it's [3]....................................... .
Camp guide And what about these trainers?
Maria They're [4]......................................., sir.
Camp guide Right, here you go, Maria. And these maps belong to the Hart twins, right?
Tony No, they aren't [5]....................................... . They're Anita's. [6]....................................... are much older.

▶ SB p. 99

Word File

At home / Around the house

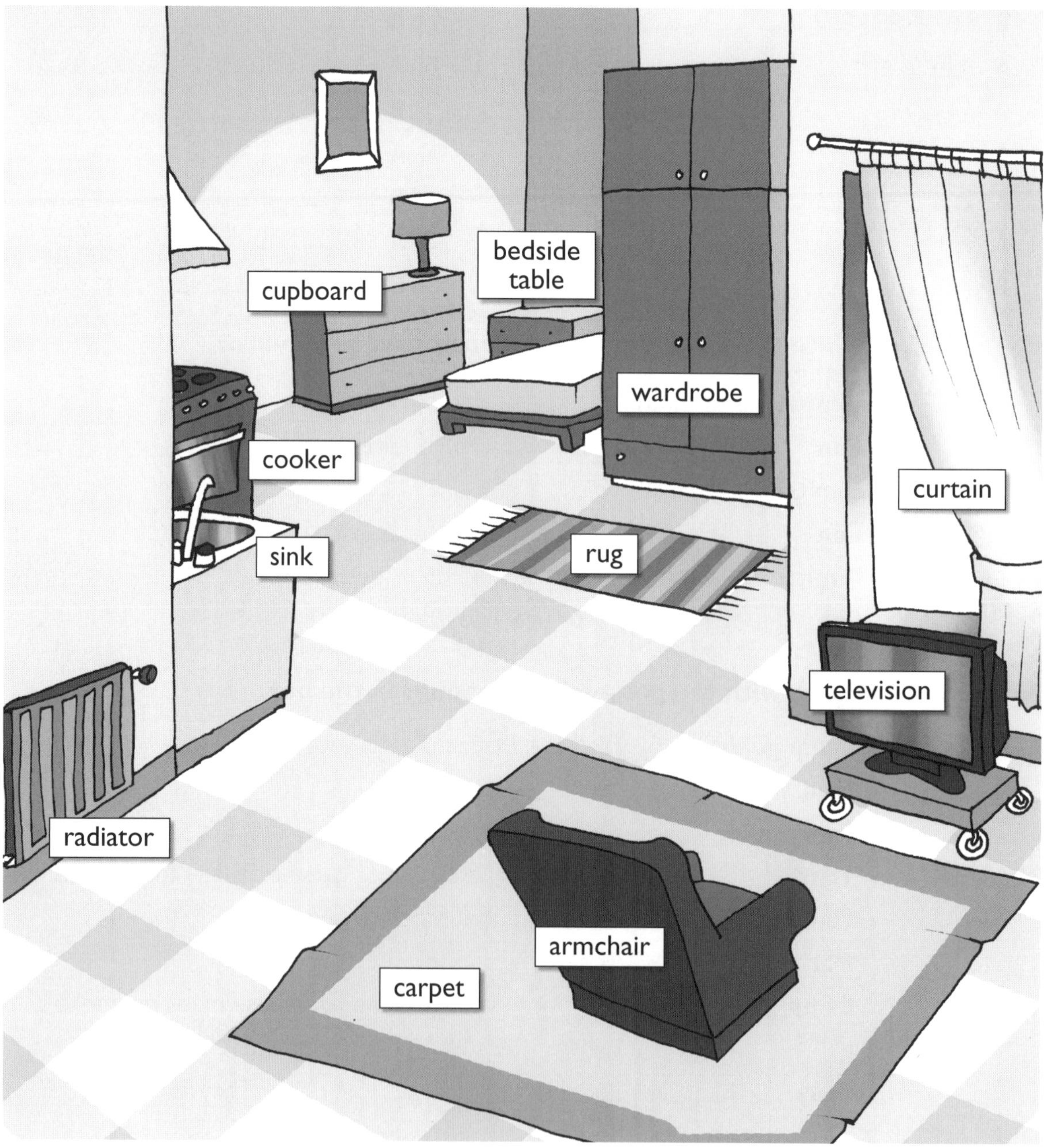

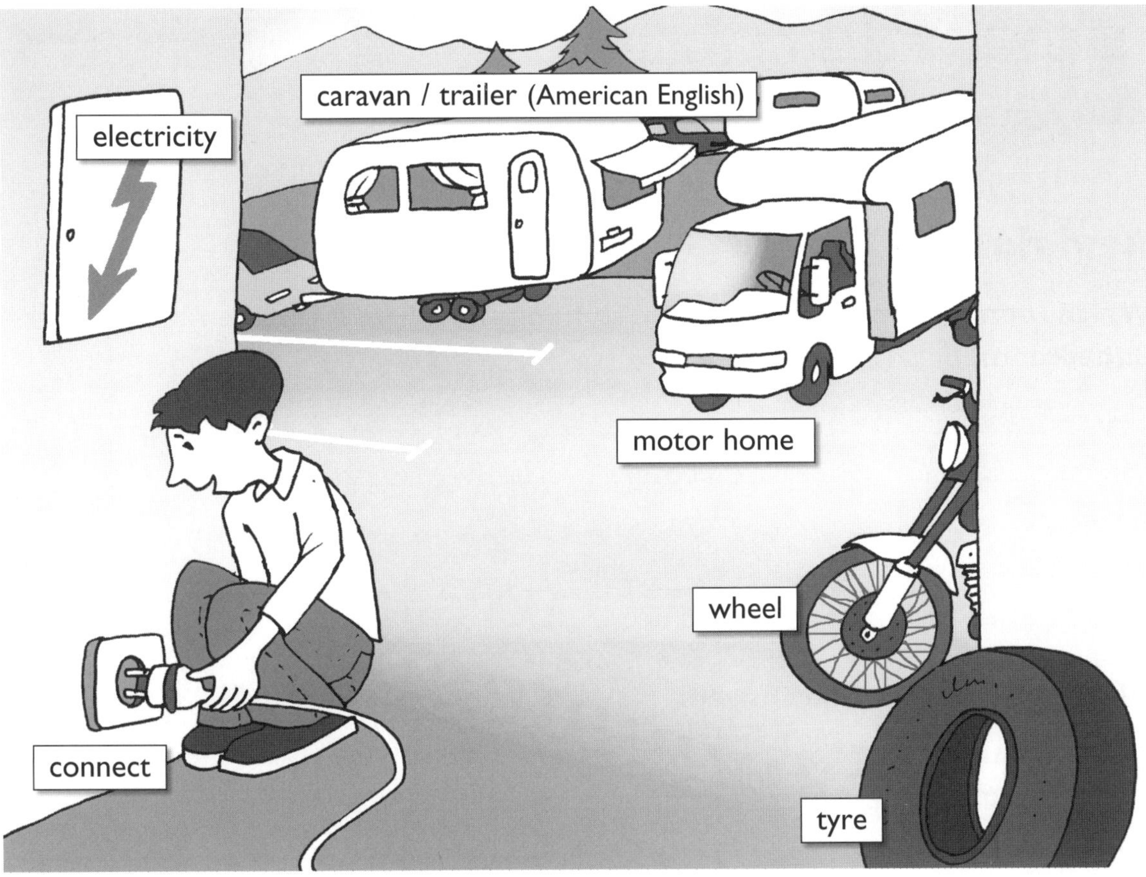

Possessive pronouns

MORE Words and Phrases

1	**heat**	*We can't play football in this heat.*	Hitze
7	**conversation**	*I had an interesting conversation with Joe last night.*	Gespräch, Unterhaltung
	share	*I want to share it with you.*	teilen
	dictionary	*This word is not in my dictionary.*	Wörterbuch
	next door	*The people next door are friendly.*	nebenan
8	**whose**	*Whose computer is this? It's not mine!*	wessen
12	**look** into	*We can look into the garden.*	hineinschauen

UNIT 15 Feeling better

Revision

● 1 **Which rooms do you usually find these things in? Write *K* (kitchen), *B* (bedroom) or *L* (living room).**

a carpet B / L	a rug	a radiator ....
a sofa	a cupboard	an armchair ....
a sink	curtains	a cooker ....
a bed	a bedside table	a lamp ....
a fridge	a wardrobe	

● 2 **Write the questions and answers.**

1 **A** Whose car is it?
B It's Mr Summer's.

2 **A** .... ?
B ....

3 **A** .... ?
B ....

4 **A** .... ?
B ....

5 **A** .... ?
B ....

6 **A** .... ?
B ....

■ 3 **Complete the sentences with the correct pronouns.**

1 **A** Go on. Take them. They're ....

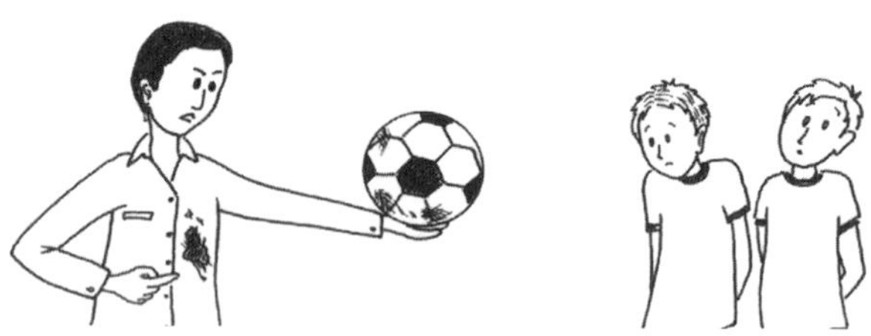

2 **A** Is this .... football?
B No, it's not ....

3 **A** It's not .... It's ....

4 **A** Whose is this dog?
B Ask Mrs Smith. I think it's ....

END OF REVISION SECTION

■ **4** **Remember the story *The pink pill* on page 100 of the Student's Book. Write sentences.**

On Monday Mr Wilkins *had a headache. His doctor gave him a yellow pill.* .

On Tuesday Mr Wilkins ....

On Wednesday Mr Wilkins ....

And on ....

■ **5** **Put the summary of the story in the correct order.**

- [ ] a headache. The doctor gave him a yellow pill but
- [ ] but the doctor still didn't give him a pink pill.
- [ ] didn't want any more pills at all.
- [ ] Mr Wilkins wasn't very happy because he wanted a pink
- [ ] left the doctor's, a man on a bike hit him. Then Mr Wilkins
- [1] On Monday Mr Wilkins went to the doctor with
- [ ] On Thursday Mr Wilkins was very happy because
- [ ] one. On the next two days he went back with different problems
- [ ] the doctor gave him a pink pill at last. But when he

● **6** **Do the crossword.**

Across:

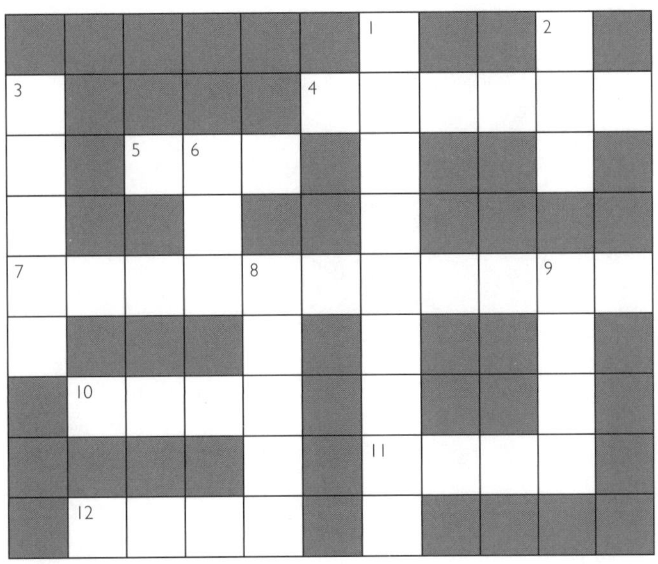

Down:

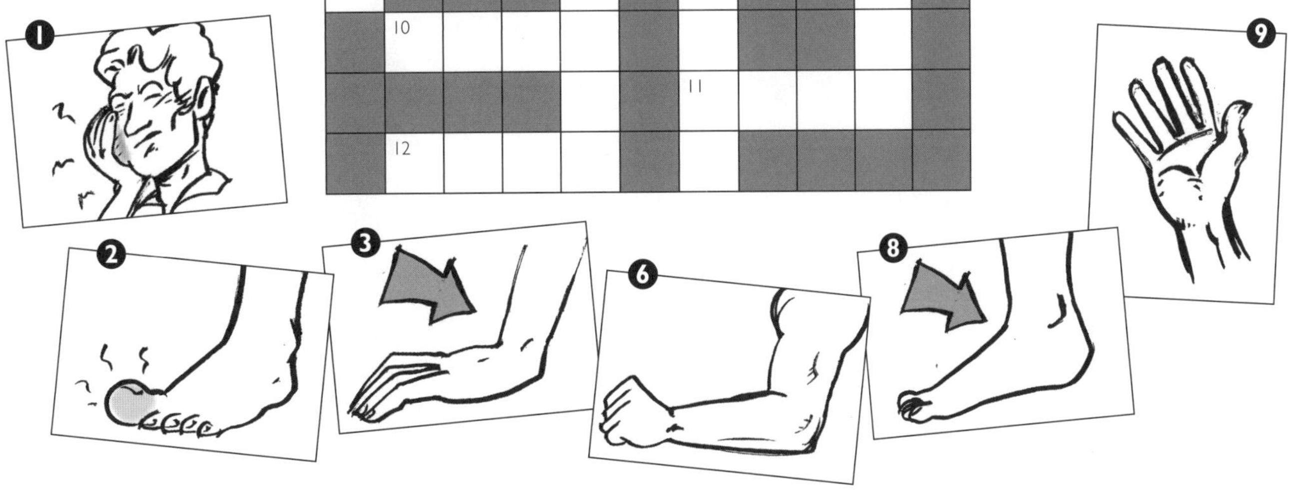

▶ SB p. 101

■ **7** **Write the words in the correct order to complete the doctor's conversations.**

1	**Doctor**	you / How / today / are / ? *How are you today?*
	Amanda	ankle / My / bit. / hurts / a ....
2	**Doctor**	your / Does / hurt / leg / ? ....
	Bartholomew	knee. / it's / No, / my / just ....
3	**Doctor**	matter / What's / the / ? ....
	Sebastian	a / back. / my / I've / got / in / pain ....
4	**Doctor**	you / better / today / Do / feel / ? ....
	Fatima	headache. / No, / a / got / still / I've ....

● **8** **Match the sentences and pictures.**

1 He's fallen off his bike.
2 She's walked into a lamp post.
3 I've cut my leg.
4 I've hurt my wrist.
5 I've eaten too much!
6 She's hurt her back.
7 He's hurt his toe.
8 I think I've broken my ankle.

▶ SB p. **102**

● **9** **Put the numbers in the correct places. Then check in the Student's Book on page 103. There are two numbers you don't need.**

10,000,000
500
20
2,000
20,000
25
200,000

1 The Amazon rainforest produces ....% of the world's oxygen.
2 Over .... plants in the rainforest can help against cancer.
3 These days there are only about .... Indians in the Amazon.
4 There were about .... Indians in the Amazon rainforest – but that was .... years ago.

■ **10** **Write one word each time to complete the text.**

The Amazon [1].......... in South America is in the middle of a rainforest. There is a big problem in the rainforest – people cut down the [2].......... because they want to make a lot of [3].......... very quickly.
The Amazon is a very important place for two reasons. First, it is the place where a lot of the world's oxygen comes from.

Second, there are thousands of [4].......... that are important for making [5].......... that can help against illnesses like cancer. Indian medicine men know how to use the plants to make the medicines. But now there are not very many medicine men, and they are very old. It is important for the [6].......... that we learn what they know!

■ **11** **Read the notes and write the names by the pictures.**

❶ *Dear Ms Jones,*
I'm sorry but Jimmy can't come to school today because he has lost his pet snake. Now he has to find it.

❷ *Dear Mr Cartwright,*
Michael can't come to school – he has a very bad stomach ache. The doctor says he must stay at home.

❸ *Dear Ms Hamilton,*
Please excuse my son Gordon from school for the next few days. He has gone to Hollywood because he wants to be a film star.

a ....

b ....

c ....

★ **12** **Imagine you are a parent. Write two notes for children who cannot go to school.**

Dear ....,
Please excuse my ....
....
He/She ....
....

....
....
....
....
....

Grammar Present perfect

■ 13 **Find ten past participles. Look in all directions.**

....

....

....

....

....

T	O	P	B	R	O	K	E	N
H	H	A	F	T	E	N	A	R
E	S	O	O	T	N	O	T	O
R	T	R	U	H	N	W	N	C
E	R	O	N	G	O	N	E	Y
T	A	H	D	U	H	G	L	P
H	Y	T	L	O	S	T	L	E
A	E	F	E	B	E	E	A	L
B	R	O	K	N	E	F	F	S

■ 14 **Complete with the words in the box.**

passed
broken
bought
gone
fallen
met

Hi Arnold,

How are things? I hope you're well. I'm writing with all the news about our family. Do you remember my brother Joshua? He has [1]............................ a guitar and now he plays music really loudly all the time. He wants to start a rock band! My father has [2]............................ his arm. He went to sleep on the sofa and fell off! He can't go to work so he's very sad. My aunt and uncle have [3]............................ on holiday – to Iceland! My sister Patricia has [4]............................ her driving test. Now she drives round and round the town – she never stops! My other brother, Hamilton, has [5]............................ a girl from Japan and has [6]............................ in love with her. Now he's learning the language – he wants to go and live in Tokyo! And me? Well, I'm going to leave home. My family are completely mad!!

Lots of love, Rachel

★ 15 **Complete with the correct form of one of the verbs in the box.**

break
eat
pass
want
go
fall

1 There's nothing left. The dog .... it all.

2 I .... my tests!!

3 Sorry, Jane isn't here. She .... into town.

4 I think I .... my toe.

5 Dad! Quickly! Jimmy .... out of the tree!

6 Oh, thanks, Grandma. I .... always .... one of these.

▶ SB p. 105

Word File

Aches

MORE Words and Phrases

1	cancer	*Some plants can help against cancer.*	Krebs
	disappointed	*I am very disappointed.*	enttäuscht
	as well	*Now I've got earache as well.*	auch, ebenfalls
	watch out	*He shouted "Watch out" but it was too late.*	pass auf
5	**drop**	*Don't drop that apple!*	fallen lassen
	That's a shame.		Wie schade! So ein Jammer!
9	rainforest	*The rainforest is a wonderful place.*	Regenwald
	sick	*I was sick yesterday.*	krank
	Indian	*The Indians in the rainforest know a lot about plants.*	Indianer/in; indianisch
	less (than)	*It takes less than 10 minutes to get there.*	weniger (als)
10	**produce**	*We produce mobile phones here.*	erzeugen
12	**final**	*Now they're in the final.*	Finale
	think about	*Think about us on Saturday.*	über etwas nachdenken; hier: an etwas denken
G	**pass** (a test)	*I want to pass this test!*	(eine Prüfung) bestehen
	lose	*I've lost my cat.*	verlieren
DVD	Let's see …		mal sehen …
	Who cares?		wen interessiert's!; wen kümmert's!
	I have no clue.		Ich habe null Ahnung.

Show what you know Units 11–15

What I CAN DO in English

This page helps you to find out how well you are doing.
Read the statements and draw symbols.

☺ = I'm good at this   ✓ = I can do this with help   ☹ = I need to practise this more

Note:
Wenn du im Buch nachschauen willst, dann helfen dir die Seitenzahlen. Das zeigen sie dir an:

Words

- ◯ I know the irregular plural forms of some words, e.g. *man/men*. (11/77)
- ◯ I can name five family members, e.g. *grandfather*. (12/82)
- ◯ I can name eight free-time activities, e.g. *dancing*. (12/83)
- ◯ I can name 12 things in rooms in a house, e.g. *chair*. (Unit 14)
- ◯ I can use possessives to say who things belong to, e.g. *mine*. (Unit 14)
- ◯ I can name five illnesses, e.g. *headache*. (Unit 15)

Speaking

- ◯ I can tell other people about activities I like doing. (12/83)
- ◯ I can have conversations about things you *must / mustn't do*. (12/85)
- ◯ I can act out a sketch. (13/88-89)
- ◯ I can talk about the things that are in a room and where they are. (Unit 14)
- ◯ I can talk about health problems. (Unit 15)

Reading and listening

- ◯ I can read and understand the text about life in Ancient Egypt. (11/77)
- ◯ I can listen to and understand the story that takes place in a pyramid. (11/79)
- ◯ I can read and understand the articles about large families. (12/82, 83)
- ◯ I can read and understand texts about different kinds of family. (12/84)
- ◯ I can read and understand a poem and put pictures in the right order. (13/88)
- ◯ I can listen to and understand a sketch about a school for ghosts. (13/88-89)
- ◯ I can read and understand a story about a magic trick. (13/90-91)
- ◯ I can read and understand texts about different kinds of homes. (14/94)
- ◯ I can listen to conversations and say where people are in the house. (14/96)
- ◯ I can read and understand the story *The pink pill*. (15/100-101)
- ◯ I can read and understand the text about plants in the Amazon rainforest. (15/103)

Writing for my Portfolio

- ◯ I have written my ending to the story *The curse of the pharaoh*. (11/81)
- ◯ I have written the rules of my school. (12/87)
- ◯ I have written a ghost story based on pictures. (13/92)
- ◯ I have written a text about either my ideal room, or the best place in my house. (14/97)
- ◯ I have written a letter to a classmate who is ill. (15/104)

UNIT 16 Virtual worlds

Revision

1 Complete with the words in the box.

ache	hurts
ankle	matter
broken	pain

1 **A** Are you OK?
B Not really. I've got a [1]................................ in my leg.

2 **A** Does your [2]................................ hurt?
B Yes. I think I've [3]................................ it.

3 **A** I've eaten too much.
B Me too. And now I've got stomach [4]................................ .

4 **A** What's the [5]................................?
B My wrist [6]................................ .

2 Find the ten verbs in the word snake. Write the past participles.

breakeatfallgomeetbuythinkknowseefind

1 ....break.......... – ....broken..........
2 .... – ....
3 .... – ....
4 .... – ....
5 .... – ....
6 .... – ....
7 .... – ....
8 .... – ....
9 .... – ....
10 .... – ....

3 Write the verb in brackets in the correct form of the present perfect.

1 They aren't here. They.....'ve..... just .....gone..... to the shopping centre. (go)
2 The lesson .... just ....! (finish)
3 My parents .... a new car. (buy)
4 I .... just .... £50 in the street! (find)
5 Oh no! My brother .... in love again! (fall)
6 I think they .... a ghost! (see)

4 Match the sentences from 3 with the pictures.

END OF REVISION SECTION

■ **5** **Complete the dialogues with sentences or phrases from the box. There are two sentences or phrases you don't need.**

Have you seen the graphics for the car races?
I've already asked my mum
~~I haven't seen the latest one yet~~
I've bought another *Potter* game.
Have you seen the battle
The Quidditch game is cool.

Dialogue 1

Micky Have you played any of the *Star Wars* games yet?

Laurie Which ones? The ones from LEGO?

Micky Yes. [1] ...... I haven't see the latest one yet ...... but I think the others were quite good.

Laurie Well, the last one is brilliant. I spent a long time on it last week. You can use the Force and it's got more than 30 characters you can choose from.

Micky Sounds great. [2] .... to buy it for me.

Laurie Come over to my place. You can try it out!

Micky Great. Thanks.

Dialogue 2

Helen What do you think of the new *Harry Potter* game?

Luke It's quite good, but I haven't tried everything out yet. [3] ....

Helen Yeah, that's really good. [4] .... against Voldemort yet?

Luke Not yet. But I'm going to in the afternoon.

Helen Let me know what you think of it.

Luke Sure, I'll email you.

★ **6** **Put the text in the correct order.**

Quidditch

- ☐ balls at the same time. Players can choose from the four Hogwarts
- ☐ Quidditch World Cup.
- ☐ House teams and will control every position on their
- [1] Fly through the air and play Quidditch, the favourite
- ☐ sport of witches and wizards. There are two
- ☐ team. They can also play international games in a World
- ☐ teams of seven players who fly around and chase four

▶ SB p. 110

★ **7** **Read the summary of *gameworld.doc*. Find the four sentences that are not from the story.**

Wakarimaska is a fantasy gaming world, and more than 30,000 people play the game. Three of the players are Ron, Julian and Janet. One day Janet sends mails from the Forest of Doom. There is a strong wind there. She can't get out of the gaming world. Julian wants to find out what is wrong. They meet a boy, Colin. His sister works in a music shop. Colin says that he has seen a strange woman go into a cave. He takes them to the cave. Suddenly Julian and Janet aren't there anymore. Ron sees Colin change into a woman and runs away. He bumps into a tree. He comes back to the real world. Julian is in his chair, but he is sleeping. Ron phones the Gamemasters and asks them for help. A woman says they will send somebody over to help him. It's four o'clock. A little bit later the doorbell rings and the woman from the cave is standing in front of Ron.

■ **8** **Write the correct verb form.**

go
think
put up
wait

Colin 1 .... you 2 .... the sign yet?
Ron Yes, I have. Where are Janet and Julian?
Colin They 3 .... already 4 .... to the next part of the cave.
Ron Have they? Why didn't they 5 .... for me?
Colin I don't know. Just follow me, I'll take you to them.
Ron Hang on a minute. I 6 .... something's wrong.
Colin Oh yes? Why do you think so, Ron?

■ **9** **Write the words in the correct order to make sentences.**

1 computer / I / games. / love

....

2 fun / You / them. / of / can / a / have / with / lot

....

3 you / And / games. / enjoy / playing

....

4 computer / really / I'm / against / games.

....

5 and / I / stupid. / they're / terrible / think

....

6 do / people / books. / should / read / sport / Young / or

....

▶ SB p. 113

Grammar Present perfect with *yet / already*

● **10 Match the pictures with the sentences.**

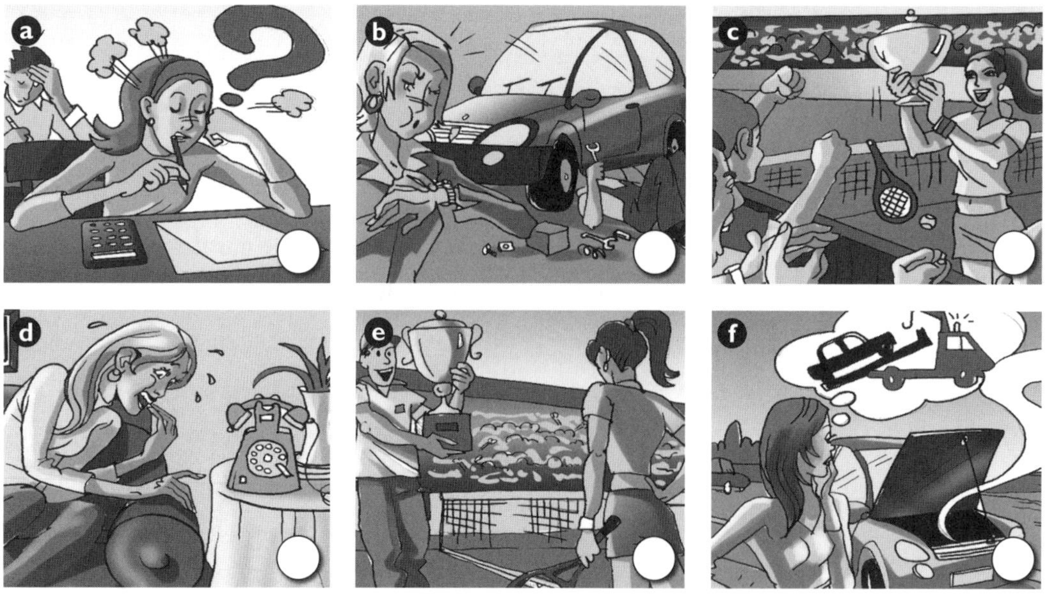

1 She has already got the trophy*.
2 They haven't phoned her yet.
3 She hasn't found the answer yet.
4 She has already phoned for help.
5 The mechanic* hasn't fixed* her car yet.
6 She hasn't got the trophy yet.

Vocabulary: *trophy – Pokal / mechanic – Mechaniker / fix – reparieren

■ **11 Write the questions. Then match the questions and answers.**

Vocabulary: *puppy – Welpe

Example:

1 he / do his homework
Has he done his homework yet? .... [g] *No he hasn't. He's still working it out.*

2 you / see the new Indiana Jones film
.... [ ] ....

3 we / arrive
.... [ ] ....

4 they / build the new hospital
.... [ ] ....

5 Harriet's dog / have puppies*
.... [ ] ....

6 she / get a new boyfriend
.... [ ] ....

7 you / sell your bicycle
.... [ ] ....

8 Dad / finish cooking dinner
.... [ ] ....

a) No, I haven't. Nobody wants it.
b) No, I haven't. Is it on already?
c) Yes, he has. We can eat in 10 minutes.
d) Yes, they have. They opened it a year ago.
e) Another 10 minutes, then we're there.
f) Yes, she has. His name's Bernie.
~~g) No he hasn't. He's still working it out.~~
h) Yes, she has. Do you want one?

▶ SB p. 115

■ **12** **Write the verbs in brackets in the correct present perfect form.**

Dialogue 1

Arnie [1]................................ you .... (play) the new *Speed* game yet?

Jamie No. In fact I [2]................................ (not see) it. [3]................................ you .... (play) it?

Arnie Yes, I have. It's awesome.

Jamie Good. I [4]................................ (heard) a lot about it.

Dialogue 2

Sue Can I borrow your latest *Dragon* game?

Matthew Sure, I [5]................................ (already play) it at least twenty times.

Sue Thanks.

Matthew Have you got *Whacky Wizard 3*?

Sue Sorry no, I [6]................................ .... (not buy) it yet. Maybe tomorrow.

★ **13** **Complete the texts with the present perfect. Then write a text of your own.**

I ...'ve logged............ (log) in.
I [1]................................ (send) you twelve emails.
I [2]................................ (try) to phone you.
I [3]................................ (send) you a fax.
And I've forgotten that you're on holiday in a mountain hut.

I [4]................................
(not do) my homework yet.
I [5]................................
(not clean out) my hamster's cage yet.
I [6]................................
(not tidy up) my room yet.
I [7]................................
(not walk) the dog yet.
But I [8]................................
(already watch) two *Simpsons* DVDs.

■ **14** **Read the poem and complete with the rhyme words in the box.**

stay
Rome
way
home

Going places

I haven't been to London yet
I haven't been to [1]................................ ,
I haven't been to Moscow yet
I've always stayed at [2]................................ .

I haven't learnt the languages
That's why I want to [3]................................ .
But when I've studied *MORE!* enough,
Then I'll be on my [4]................................ .

▶ SB p. 115

Word File

Computer words

virtual
graphics
portal
service desk
control
level
multiplayer mode
log in
log out
online
offline

MORE Words and Phrases

1	create	*You can create your team.*	erstellen, schaffen
	come around	*Can you come around tomorrow?*	vorbeikommen
	(be) set	*This game is set in the African jungle.*	spielen
	rescue	*They rescued some animals.*	retten
	awesome	*This game is awesome.*	wunderbar, toll
	graphics	*The graphics of this game are cool.*	Grafik
	part	*He is part African. His family is from Kenya.*	teilweise, teils
	part	*You can play the part of the king.*	Rolle
	at the moment	*I'm playing another game at the moment.*	im Moment
	ever	*Have you ever got lost?*	je
	think of	*What do you think of the new Pirate Ahoy game?*	halten von
2	weird	*That's a really weird game.*	merkwürdig, seltsam, komisch
	helmet	*I've lost my helmet – can I borrow yours?*	Helm
	role	*He likes his new role.*	Rolle
	What's up?	*What's up? I don't know – he won't wake up!*	Was ist los?
	harmless	*That dog is harmless.*	harmlos
	cave	*This cave looks very dark.*	Höhle
	queen	*The queen isn't a very friendly person.*	Königin
	(not) any longer	*He didn't look like a boy any longer.*	nicht mehr
	follow me		folge mir
	future	*I'm the future queen.*	Zukunft
	hang on	*Hang on a minute.*	warte mal
3	**without**	*Can I have my coffee without milk?*	ohne
4	flash	*The colours are flashing.*	blitzen
	skill	*He played with great skill.*	Geschick; hier: Fähigkeit, Fertigkeit
	outer space	*I dreamt I was in outer space.*	Weltraum, Weltall
	forbid	*My parents have forbidden me to go out this weekend.*	verbieten
	endless		endlos
	battle	*Some computer games are full of fights and battles and shootings.*	Kampf, Schlacht
	shooting		Erschießung
	fight		Kampf, Streit
	powerful	*Somebody very powerful is after you.*	mächtig
	speed	*I like the speed in car games.*	Geschwindigkeit
5	**not ... yet**	*I haven't seen it yet.*	noch nicht
6	motorbike	*I like racing around on cars or motorbikes.*	Motorrad
	race		rennen, rasen
	fight	*You fight on four levels.*	kämpfen

UNIT 17 Caring for animals

Revision

● 1 **Find eight words from the story *gameworld.doc*. Look in all directions.**

....
....
....
....

Q	U	F	O	R	E	S	T
N	P	T	E	M	L	E	H
G	O	E	A	A	T	R	Q
I	R	E	V	R	S	V	U
S	T	J	V	A	A	A	E
N	A	S	T	I	C	N	E
E	L	O	R	T	W	T	N

● 2 **Write the verbs in brackets in the present perfect.**

Dialogue 1

Andy 1................................ you .... (be) to London yet?

Liz Yes, I 2.. (already be) there twice.

Andy What do you think of it?

Liz Well, I 3.. (not see) all the sights, but I think it's a great city.

Dialogue 2

Dad 4................................ you .... (study) for your test yet?

Annie No, I 5................................ .

Dad But I 6.. (already tell) you three times!

Annie I know. I 7.. (not forget). I'm going to start tomorrow.

Dad OK then.

★ 3 **Complete the email from Nicola with the correct present perfect forms. Then find a name for the puppy.**

Hi Mario,
I'm not sure you 1................................ (heard) about this, but my mum 2................................ (buy) a little puppy for me. It's so sweet with its white fur* and little black spots*! I 3................................ (have) it for 2 weeks now, and it 4................................ (be) a fantastic time! But now I need your help! I 5................................ (not think) of a name for the puppy yet. My sister Claire 6................................ (try) to find a name too, and she 7................................ (make) three suggestions: Lollipop, Hannibal and President!!! But I hate them. Yuck! ☹
Please find a good name for my little puppy!
Love, Nicola

I think the best name for Nicola's puppy would be:

....

Vocabulary: *fur – Fell / spot – Fleck, dunkle Stelle

END OF REVISION SECTION

4 Complete the sentences with the word in the box.

walking
brushing
feeding
cleaning out
stroking

1 Susie is .... her pet.

2 Susie is .... her pet.

3 Susie is .... her pet's cage.

4 Susie is .... her pet.

5 Susie is .... her pet.

5 Read the interview and write the questions.

1 How often do you feed it?
2 What does it eat?
3 And where does it live?
4 Where does it come from?
5 And what colour is it?
6 Is it a difficult pet to keep?

Interviewer Daniel, you've got an unusual pet. Tell us more about it.

Daniel It's a chameleon.

Interviewer Wow, a chameleon. [1]..

Daniel Chameleons live in many different countries but mine comes from Madagascar.

Interviewer [2]..

Daniel It's usually green but when it gets angry it changes colour to red. It can change colour to orange and yellow, too. But I don't know why.

Interviewer [3]..

Daniel No. It's quite easy really. I mean you don't have to give it a bath or anything like that. You just have to give it food and clean its glass tank once a week.

Interviewer [4]..

Daniel Just once a day.

Interviewer [5]..

Daniel Insects and things like that.

Interviewer [6]..

Daniel In a big glass tank. It's about 2 m high and 1 m wide. It's got a tree in it.

▶ SB p. 117

■ **6** **Read the interview again and circle T (*True*) or F (*False*).**

1 You can only find chameleons in Madagascar. T / F
2 Daniel's chameleon changes to red when it's angry. T / F
3 His chameleon doesn't need a bath. T / F
4 Daniel cleans the tank every day. T / F
5 The chameleon eats insects. T / F
6 The chameleon lives in a tree in the garden. T / F

● **7** **Write *Wallace*, *Rover* or both names next to the sentences. Check with the sketch *Small talk between dogs* on page 118 of the Student's Book.**

1 He has to walk his owner twice a day. ....
2 He's got a lot of friends in the park. ....
3 He doesn't like Admiral. ....
4 He's run away from his owner. ....
5 He doesn't like his owner stroking him. ....
6 He hasn't seen a good TV programme for a long time. ....
7 His owner is not a good driver. ....
8 His owner is shouting for him. ....

● **8** **Look at the picture and choose the sentence you like the best.**

1 "I'm sure I've been here before."
2 "I think I need a new hobby."
3 "This is fun!"

★ **9** **What do you think these pets are thinking? Write a sentence for each one.**

★ **10** **Read the stories and put the sentences or phrases in the correct places.**

Norman the Dog

Norman is a Labrador. He is blind. He lived in a dog sanctuary* until one day Annette came and gave him a home. One day Annette and Norman were on the beach. [2] Suddenly Norman started running. He heard something that nobody else could hear [ ] The dog jumped into the sea and swam towards the screams. He found the girl and pulled her back to the beach. Norman saved the little girl's life.

RINGO THE CAT

Ray and Carol were in bed. Both of them had headaches and they were very tired. Their cat Ringo wanted to go outside so Carol got up and opened the door. [ ] He looked at Carol. She understood this look and followed him into the garden. Ringo started digging and Carol smelt gas. She called the gas company*. [ ] The company told Ray and Carol that the gas leak* was very dangerous. Ringo saved their lives.

Lulu the Pig

Sue has an unusual pet called Lulu. Lulu is a pig. One day Sue went away for a few days, her mother JoAnn went to Sue's house to look after Lulu. Suddenly, JoAnn had a heart attack* and fell on the floor. [ ] She ran into the street and sat in the middle of the road to stop the cars. A car stopped. The driver followed the little pig into the house and found JoAnn on the floor. [ ] JoAnn was taken to hospital. The little pig saved her life.

1 But Ringo didn't want to go outside on his own.
2 ~~The beach is the only place where Norman can run freely because he is blind.~~
3 Lulu knew something was wrong.
4 – the sound of a young girl screaming.
5 They arrived and solved the problem.
6 He called for an ambulance.

Vocabulary: * sanctuary – Tierheim / company – Gesellschaft / gas leak – undichte Stelle in einer Gasleitung / heart attack – Herzinfakt

★ **11** **Write a short story about a clever animal. Finish the story with the words …** ***saved my life.***

....

....

....

....

▶ SB p. 120

Grammar *So do I / Neither do I*

■ **12 Complete with the sentences in the box.**

So do I.
So have I.
So have I.
Neither do I.
Neither have I.
Neither have I.

1 **A** I really like punk music.
B ....

2 **A** I've got a problem.
B ....

3 **A** I haven't seen this film yet.
B ....

4 **A** I've already done my homework.
B ....

5 **A** I don't want to go to school today.
B ....

6 **A** I haven't got any money.
B ....

★ **13 Complete the dialogues. Begin with *So* or *Neither*.**

1 **A** I live in Rotterdam.
B So do .... I.

2 **A** Daniel's got an MP3-player.
B .... I.

3 **A** I don't know what to do.
B .... I.

4 **A** I've never been to Paris.
B .... I.

5 **A** I want to go home.
B .... I.

6 **A** I've lost my homework.
B .... I.

★ **14 Which of these sentences are also true for you? Write *So … I.* or *Neither … I.* next to the true ones and then compare with a partner.**

1 I love football. ....

2 I read a lot of magazines. ....

3 I think hip-hop is great. ....

4 I haven't been to England. ....

5 I've got a pet. ....

6 I don't like Maths. ....

7 I haven't got a laptop. ....

8 I've met a famous person. ....

▶ SB p. 121

Word File

Living with animals

MORE Words and Phrases

1	**dry**	*You must keep your pet dry and clean.*	trocknen
7	boss sb around (informal)	*Don't boss me around!*	herumkommandieren
	Neither do I.	*'I don't like cats.' 'Neither do I.'*	Ich auch nicht.
	behave	*Teach your dog how to behave.*	benehmen
	such	*He's such a bad driver.*	solch, e, r, s
	while	*She wants to stroke me while she's watching TV.*	während
9	peaceful	*On a farm, it can be very peaceful.*	friedlich; friedfertig
	care for	*You should care for your horse.*	sich kümmern um
	cruelty	*I hate cruelty to animals.*	Grausamkeit
	healthy	*Good food makes you healthy.*	gesund
	state	*The farm is in the state of Virginia.*	Staat

UNIT 18 Get active!

Revision

1 Here are six things you should do with a pet. Match to make sentences.

1 You should take	☐ it.
2 You should clean out	☐ it.
3 You should feed	☐ it to the vet.
4 You should play	☐ it a bath.
5 You should give	☐ its cage.
6 You should walk	☐ with it.

2 Circle the correct answer.

1 **A** I don't like this food.
B *So do I. / Neither do I.*

2 **A** I like being here.
B *So do I. / Neither do I.*

3 **A** I hate spiders!
B *So do I. / Neither do I.*

4 **A** I don't clean out my pet's cage.
B *So do I. / Neither do I.*

5 **A** I haven't got a bike.
B *So have I. / Neither have I.*

6 **A** I've got three pets.
B *So have I. / Neither have I.*

7 **A** I've been to New York.
B *So have I. / Neither have I.*

8 **A** I haven't seen that film.
B *So have I. / Neither have I.*

3 Read the sentences below. Write what's true for you. Use *So do I.*, *I don't.*, *Neither do I.* or *I do.*

1 I like playing volleyball.

....

2 I watch a lot of television.

....

3 I never go to bed before half past nine.

....

4 I never want to live in another country.

....

5 I like listening to music.

....

6 I always tidy my room.

....

7 I often help mum or dad with the cooking.

....

8 On Saturdays I often go shopping with mum or dad.

....

END OF REVISION SECTION

● 4 Find the odd one out.

1 football tennis basketball volleyball
2 surfing swimming running windsurfing
3 tennis cycling swimming snowboarding
4 skiing football mountain climbing snowboarding
5 skateboarding snowboarding surfing ice skating

● 5 Which sport(s) are they talking about?

1 I usually play in the summer – it's too cold in the winter. It's good because you only need two people. But sometimes you can play with four people, of course.

....

2 I love this sport! You can play indoors but I like playing it on the beach. All you need is a net and a ball – but even on the beach you need four people to play. But that isn't usually a problem.

....

3 This is the best sport in the world because all you need is a pair of good trainers and off you go! No special equipment* and you don't even need other people!

....

4 The first time I did this sport I hated it because I got so cold! But in the summer the weather is warmer and then it's great to be in the warm water! I go with my friends now, at the weekends. The board's a bit expensive, but that's all.

....

5 My favourite sport is a problem for me because there aren't any mountains where I live. So I have to go to another country. And I can only do it in winter! It's difficult and the boards are expensive, but I still love it!

....

Vocabulary: *equipment – Ausrüstung

■ 6 Complete the dialogue with the words in the box.

tennis
twice
favourite
game
often
sports

Nicole	What's your 1.................................. sport, Matthew?
Matthew	Hmm, probably basketball. But I like 2.................................. too.
Nicole	Are you a good player?
Matthew	I'm not bad.
Nicole	How 3.................................. do you play?
Matthew	Well, I play tennis 4.................................. a week and basketball four times a week. I'm in the school team.
Nicole	Oh really? You do a lot of sport!
Matthew	True. What about you? Do you like any 5.................................. ?
Nicole	Well, I like watching basketball on TV.
Matthew	So, would you like to watch tomorrow's 6.................................. with me?
Nicole	Sure. Why not?

▶ SB p. 123

■ **7** **Read the story and put the pictures in the correct order.**

Coach Carter*

Vocabulary: *coach – Trainer / high school – Oberstufengymnasium / grade – Note / gym – Turnhalle / headmaster – Schulleiter

Last week, I saw a film called *Coach Carter*. It's about a basketball team at Richmond High School* in the USA, who lose most of their games. And then they get a new coach – a man called Mr Carter. He makes them work very hard, they have to practise every day. And then they win some games, so they're very happy! And everything seems OK, but there's a problem: the players are also at school and they aren't working very much so they don't get good grades*. And Mr Carter locks the school gym*! Now the players can't practise. The headmaster* of the school thinks Carter is wrong and he opens the gym again. The boys can play and practise again, and the team gets to the big final – but they lose to St Francis School: 71–70 in a very exciting game. The players are very unhappy, but Coach Carter thinks they have done very well and he congratulates them. It's not a bad story.

★ **8** **Read the text about Felix Baumgartner. Write the phrases in the correct places.**

- another world record
- a bit like
- very, very quickly
- from the highest bridge
- worth it
- open their parachute
- breaking records
- only 50 metres

Austrian Felix Baumgartner

Austrian Felix Baumgartner does different sports, but he's probably most famous for base jumping. Base jumping is 1 .... parachuting, but you don't jump out of a plane. Base jumpers jump from places like buildings, bridges and mountains, and they only 2 .... at the last moment.

In 1999, Baumgartner jumped from the statue of Christ in Rio de Janeiro. He had to open his parachute 3 .... , because the jump was only 29 metres – the lowest parachute jump ever!

On June 7th, 2004, he jumped 343 metres 4 .... in the world, at Millau in France. Then in December of the same year, he was back in Rio de Janeiro – this time, he broke 5 .... when he jumped from a helicopter over Copacabana beach and opened his parachute 6 .... from the sand.

Baumgartner loves 7 .... Sometimes he has to prepare for a long time before, but he thinks it's 8 ....

▶ SB p. 125

■ **9** **Put the text about Emma Sanderson in the correct order.**

- ☐ 2002/03. She was the youngest woman to
- ☐ complete the 29,000 mile solo race, and she
- 1 Emma Sanderson, from England, is a
- ☐ famous for winning the 'Around Alone Race' in
- ☐ or alone. She won the 'Round Britain and Ireland
- ☐ Race' in 2000 when she was 25, but she is most
- ☐ telling children about her sailing.
- ☐ was alone at sea for 135 days. Now Emma enjoys
- ☐ yachtswoman. She sails a yacht, in team races

Grammar Present perfect with *ever* and *never*

■ **10** **Match the questions and answers.**

1 Have you ever met anybody famous?
2 Have you ever been on television?
3 Have you ever been to the sea?
4 Have you ever written a poem?
5 Have you ever won a competition?
6 Have you ever gone snowboarding?
7 Have you ever fallen asleep in a lesson?
8 Have you ever seen a ghost?

- ☐ No, I never have – and I'm never going to! I hate mountains and snow!
- ☐ Well, I met a footballer in a shop once, but I can't say he was really famous.
- ☐ Once. But the teacher didn't see me so it was OK.
- ☐ No, I haven't. But my mum has. She was really scared.
- ☐ Yes, I have. Two years ago I won the tennis competition at school!
- ☐ Yes, I have. And I love writing them, too.
- ☐ Yes, I have. We went swimming every day.
- ☐ No, but my sister has. She was on a quiz programme once. She lost!

▶ SB p. 126

★ **11 Complete the interview with the phrases in the box.**

ever been
never been
ever had
never had
~~ever played~~
never lost
ever broken
never broken

1 **A** Have you ....ever played.......... in the USA?
B Yes, lots of times, and I've .... a match there.

2 **A** Have you .... to the Olympic Games?
B No, I haven't. I've .... the chance to go.

3 **A** Have you .... any world records?
B No, never. And I've .... world champion.

4 **A** Have you .... a bad accident?
B Yes, lots!! I've broken both my legs but I've .... my arm.

■ **12 Write the words in the correct order to make sentences or questions.**

1 you / have / handball / ever / played / ?
Have you ever played handball?

2 Japanese* / eaten / you / have / food / ever / ?
....

3 never / I've / Olympic Games. / to / been / the
....

4 ever / you / broken / wrist / have / your / ?
....

5 competition. / never / I've / a / won
....

6 brother / my / a poem. / never / has / written
....

7 parents / never / my / have / France. / to / been
....

8 dinner / family / you / ever / have / for / your / cooked / ?
....

Vocabulary: *Japanese – japanisch

● **13 Tick the sentences that are true for you.**

1 I've never been to the USA. ☐
2 I've never played volleyball. ☐
3 I've never sailed in a yacht. ☐
4 I've never broken my arm. ☐
5 I've never had a bad accident. ☐
6 I've never eaten Chinese food. ☐

▶ SB p. **127**

Word File

Sports

cycle
bike
skate
roller-skating
ice skating
train
trainer
professional
kick
score
goalie
yachtswoman
yacht
race
sailing
trampolining
trampoline
parachute
parachuting
sportsman
sportswoman

MORE Words and Phrases

4	**grow up**	*When I grow up I want to be an Olympic skier.*	erwachsen werden; aufwachsen mit
5	**competition**	*I love taking part in competitions!*	Wettbewerb
7	**appear**	*Suddenly a ghost appeared.*	erscheinen
	fall asleep	*My dad always falls asleep in front of the TV.*	einschlafen
	nil	*In the end the score was two – nil.*	null
	rest	*I needed some rest.*	Rest; Ruhe
8	tackle	*Helen tackled Eddie.*	niederrennen
	waste of time	*I've had enough. It's waste of time.*	Zeitverschwendung
9	free fall	*In free fall you can go 60 metres a second.*	freier Fall
	height	*What height is that building?*	Höhe
	radio mast	*There is a radio mast on the tower.*	Antenne
	statue	*The statue of Christ is less than 40 m tall.*	Statue, Standbild
	fearless	*To do base jumping, you have to be fearless.*	furchtlos
	total	*You need total concentration to be a base jumper.*	gesamt; völlig
	challenge	*What will the next challenge be?*	Herausforderung
	hard	*It is hard work.*	hart, schwer
	at the time	*It was the tallest building at the time.*	zu der Zeit; damals
	wing	*He has a parachute and a carbon wing.*	Flügel
10	hurricane	*The hurricane hit Florida and destroyed many houses.*	Orkan; Hurrikan
	ocean	*The oceans cover $^2/_3$ of the Earth.*	Meer, Ozean
12	make friends	*Volleyball is a good way to make friends.*	sich anfreunden

Light rain in the north

Revision

● 1 **Write down all the names of the sports in the picture.**

....

....

....

....

....

....

....

....

....

....

....

....

....

....

....

....

....

● 2 **Match the questions and answers.**

1 Have you ever been to Italy?	☐ Yes, I have. But he can't come.
2 Have you finished that book yet?	☐ Yes, I have. But she wasn't at home.
3 Have you ever seen the Eiffel Tower?	☐ Yes. I've been to Rome and Venice.
4 Have you invited Fred to your party?	☐ No, I haven't started it yet!
5 Have you ever made breakfast?	☐ No. I've still got another 50 pages to read.
6 Have you finished your homework yet?	☐ Yes, I have. I often make it on Sundays.
7 Have you ever been surfing?	☐ No, I've never been to Paris.
8 Have you phoned Emily?	☐ No, I've never even been to the sea.

■ 3 **Write the questions for the pictures.**

1 *Have you ever seen a shark?* .... (see)

2 .... (climb)

3 .... (see)

4 .... (find)

END OF REVISION SECTION

★ **4** **Remember the formula. Circle T (*True*) or F (*False*) for the sentences.**

To convert Fahrenheit temperatures into Centigrade:

- Begin by subtracting* 32 from the Fahrenheit number.
- Divide* the answer by 9.
- Then multiply* that answer by 5.

Vocabulary: *subtract – subtrahieren
divide – dividieren / multiply – multiplizieren

1 100°C is hotter than 200°F. T / F
2 86°F is colder than 25°C. T / F
3 122°F is the same as 60°C. T / F
4 30°C is not as hot as 94°F. T / F
5 40°F is not as cold as 10°C. T / F
6 0°C is as cold as 32°F. T / F

■ **5** **Find the weather words and write them next to the symbols. (← → ↑ ↓ ↙ ↘)**

F	E	O	Q	S	C	O	L	D	R	S	R
E	O	I	U	L	A	E	A	T	U	E	A
A	Y	G	O	F	F	H	O	T	I	G	I
B	A	H	S	E	I	E	X	Q	Y	T	R
O	S	K	C	P	F	G	C	N	O	S	Y
K	D	O	L	D	U	H	N	A	K	A	D
L	I	O	O	Y	K	U	O	S	L	Z	N
O	N	W	U	N	S	O	P	N	I	C	I
O	I	W	D	N	O	I	I	O	I	D	W
R	A	A	S	U	O	L	O	W	H	S	J
M	R	O	T	S	R	E	D	N	U	H	T

Thunderstorm

cold

snow

clouds

sunny

Rain

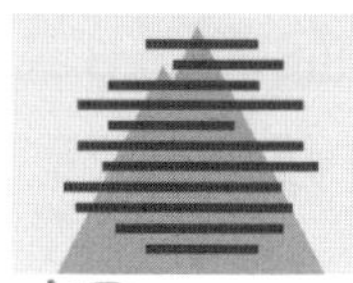
Fog

windy

Hot

■ **6** **Look at the map and write the weather forecast.**

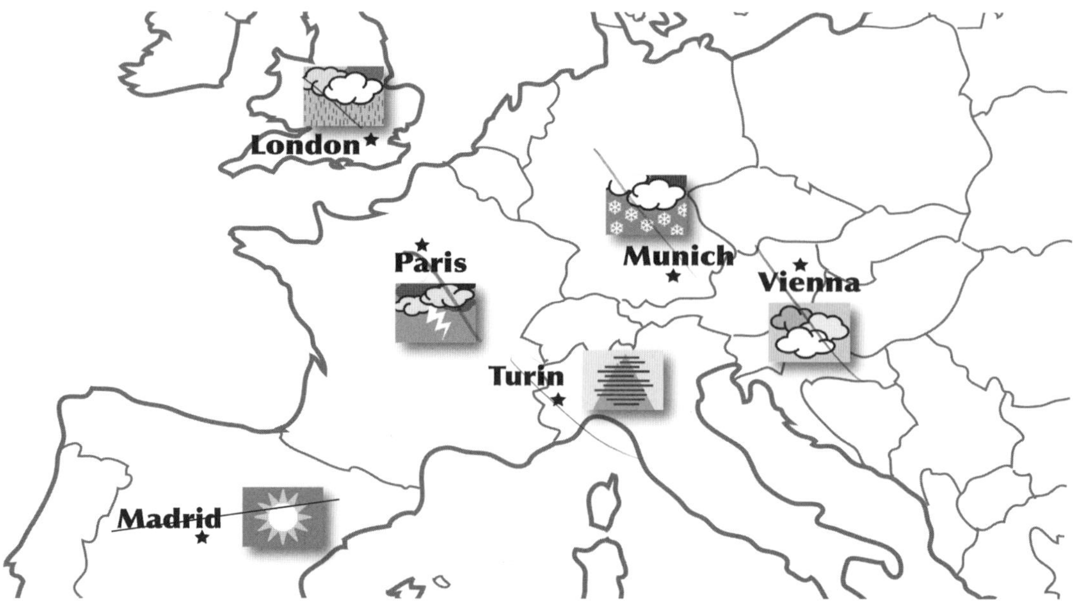

1 It will be sunny in Madrid.
2 There will be a Thunderstorm in Paris
3 It will rain in London
4 It will be foggy in Turin
5 It will be cloudy in Vienna
6 It will snow in Munich

▶ SB p. 129

★ **7** **Read the stories and write the best title for each story.**

1 Above the clouds
2 The water went away
3 Where the rain stopped

Weird weather stories

Where the rain stopped

Once when I was a young boy I was in the back garden playing football. It was a beautiful sunny day but when I looked at the sky, I saw some black clouds arriving. I went around the house to tell my mother because her washing was on the line*. When I got to the front door, it was already raining heavily. We went to the back garden again but when we got there, there was nothing but sun. It was weird. When you looked one way, there was rain. When you looked the other way, there was sun.

Above the clouds

I was on holiday in New York. It was really hot. The temperature was over 40°C. It was too hot so my friend and I went to the top of the Empire State Building. "The air will be cooler at the top," we thought. We were wrong, but there were some clouds coming towards us. The clouds brought a thunderstorm with them. But we were so high up the storm happened below us. We watched the lightning* and the rain falling but we didn't get wet. It was so weird!

Vocabulary: *lightning – Blitz
line – Wäscheleine
sandbag – Sandsack

The water went away

I was about 12. There was a river at the end of our garden. On a Thursday in October, it started to rain and rain. On the Saturday morning, I went into the garden and I saw that the river was higher than usual. The water started to come into our garden and I shouted to my mum and dad. They ran out, and my dad went to get some sandbags*. But at that moment the rain stopped and the water began to go back again. My dad came back and we watched the water go away. We were so happy, and the three of us laughed and danced around.

★ **8** **Imagine you are on holiday and took one of these photos. Choose one and write a holiday postcard to one of your friends.**

....

....

....

....

....

....

....

....

▶ SB p. 132

Grammar *will/won't*

9 Write the sentences.

I'll give you some.
~~Oh! It really hurts.~~
I'm really scared of dogs.
I've got lots of homework tonight.

I haven't got enough money.
I'll bring it tomorrow. I promise.
OK, leave it. I'll do it later.
I'll carry it for you.

~~Where's your homework?~~
I'll take you to hospital.
I'm not. I'll get it.
This suitcase* is heavy.

Vocabulary: *suitcase – Koffer

10 Match the sentences.

1 It's my birthday tomorrow.
2 The film starts at six. Don't forget!
3 How am I going to get home?
4 The car's really dirty.
5 Here's £3.
6 I'm going to miss the game on TV.
7 I'm really hungry.
8 It's cold in here.
9 The phone's ringing.
10 It's a secret.

- [8] I'll close the window.
- [10] I won't tell anybody.
- [6] OK. I'll record it for you.
- [5] Thanks. I'll give it back to you tomorrow.
- [9] I'll answer it.
- [1] I'll make a cake.
- [2] Don't worry – I'll be there.
- [4] I'll clean it for you.
- [7] I'll make you a sandwich.
- [3] My father will take you in our car.

▶ SB p. 133

★ **11** **Look at the pictures and write the people's dreams.**

1 I'll be rich one day.

2 ....

3 ....

4 ....

5 ....

6 ....

Grammar *will/might*

■ **12** **Write *might*, *'ll* or *won't*.**

1 **A** The party starts at eight, Dave.
B I know. I .... be late. I promise.

2 **A** Lunch will be ready in an hour.
B I .... help you. It'll be quicker.

3 **A** What's Mike going to do when he finishes school?
B He's not sure. He .... go to university or he .... look for a job.

4 **A** What chance have Manchester United got in the cup final?
B They .... win because they're terrible.

5 **A** Where are you going on holiday this year?
B Well, we .... go to France or we .... go to Spain.

6 **A** I only slept two hours last night.
B Well, you .... be tired later.

★ **13** **Write sentences about your future. Use *might*, *might not*, *'ll* or *won't* and the ideas in the box.**

buy a laptop get a surfboard go out with Jasmine go to the moon travel to the Amazon learn to drive be a famous scientist write a book

....

....

....

....

....

....

....

....

Word File Weather forecast

Nouns:
map
outlook (for tomorrow)
(weather) report
weatherman
temperature
scale
cloud
snow
fog
rainfall
thunderstorm
sunny spells
showers

Adjectives:
average (temperature)
rainy
wet
windy
mild
dry
northern
eastern
western
southern
cloudy
cool
clear

Verbs:
clear up
record

MORE Words and Phrases

1	formula	*The formula is C = (F-32):1.8*	Formel
2	**continue**	*The rain will continue until tomorrow.*	andauern; weitergehen
	give way	*Rain in the morning will give way to sun later on.*	ausweichen, Platz machen
	spell	*There will be some spells of sunshine between the rain showers.*	Zeit, Periode
3	make sure	*Make sure you take your umbrella!*	sich versichern, darauf achten
	mist	*Heavy mist in the Stoke area will clear up later.*	Nebel, Dunst
	thick	*Watch out! There's thick fog here.*	dick, dicht
4	raincoat	*It's raining. Take your raincoat.*	Regenmantel
	all day	*It will be sunny all day in England.*	den ganzen Tag
	Have a nice day!		Einen schönen Tag.
	rise	*The temperatures will rise to 20°C.*	steigen
5	**train**	*I'm taking the next train to London.*	Zug
6	**pack**	*Pack your bags! We're going on holiday!*	packen
	swimming trunks	*Have you packed your swimming trunks?*	Badehose
	bathing suit	*Bring your bathing suit with you.*	Badeanzug
	turn up/down	*Turn up the volume – I can't hear what they're saying.*	aufdrehen, leiser drehen
	volume	*Please don't turn up the volume.*	Lautstärke
	situation	*The situation is difficult.*	Situation, Lage
	unpack	*Unpack your bathing suit and pack your raincoat!*	auspacken
	apologise	*I apologise – I was wrong.*	sich entschuldigen
7	**generally**	*It's generally hot and sunny in Italy in the summer.*	allgemein
	throughout the year	*In the Lake District it can be rainy throughout the year.*	im ganzen Jahr
	inch (pl inches)	*England has gone metric – but they give rainfall in inches!*	Zoll (2,54 cm)
	below	*The temperature will be below 0°C tomorrow.*	unten; unterhalb
	turn sth off/on	*Jamie, turn off the TV.*	etwas aus/einschalten
	wherever	*There will be sunshine wherever we look.*	wo auch immer
8	pity	*We have to leave soon – what a pity.*	hier: schade, dass
	tan	*You have a great tan.*	(Sonnen)Bräune
	Centigrade		Celsius
	clear	*It is sunny, dry and clear.*	klar
	sea level	*Death Valley is 282 feet below sea level.*	Meeresspiegel

UNIT 20 The last week

Revision

● 1 **Match the words with the symbols.**

☐ thunderstorm ☐ snow ☐ clouds ☐ sunny ☐ rain ☐ fog

● 2 **Circle the correct answer.**

1 **A** You look tired.
B Yes, I am. I think *I'll go / I won't go* to bed.

2 **A** I'm going to give your dog some cabbage.
B He hates cabbage, so he *will / won't* eat it.

3 **A** Have you invited John to the party?
B No, *I'll / I won't* phone him after dinner.

4 **A** I'm going to ask Helen.
B Don't do that. She *will / won't* know the answer.

5 **A** I'm ready to start my homework.
B It's not much! It *won't take / will take* longer than an hour.

6 **A** Dad, I've got a problem with my homework.
B I'm busy. Ask your mother, *she'll / she won't* help you.

■ 3 **Write sentences about tomorrow's weather.**

Example:

1 *There'll be some showers in Venice.*
2 ....
3 ....
4 ....
5 ....
6 ....

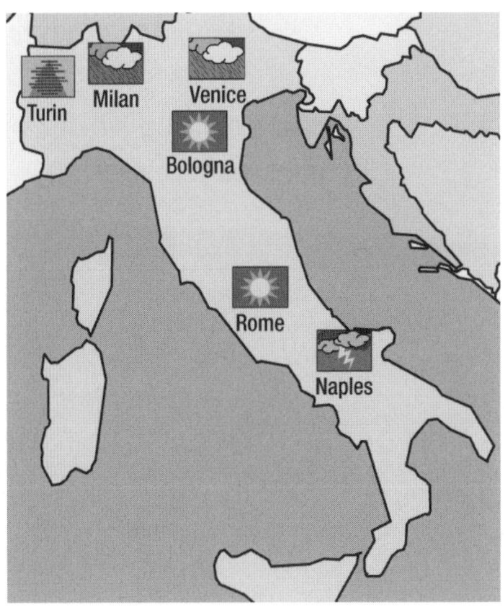

END OF REVISION SECTION

■ **4 Read the conversation between Marcus and his dad and circle T (*True*) or F (*False*).**

Marcus Dad?
Dad What is it?
Marcus I want to paint my bedroom.
Dad Good idea. It certainly needs some fresh paint. It looks terrible from all the silly posters you've put on the wall and taken off again.
Marcus What do you mean, 'silly posters'?
Dad Well, all your music posters, for example.
Marcus My music posters? Silly? You have no idea! So, can I paint my room?
Dad Sure.
Marcus Can you get me two tins of black paint then?
Dad Magic word?
Marcus Please.
Dad Hang on, did you just say 'black'?
Marcus Yes, is there a problem?
Dad There certainly is. There's no way you're going to paint your room black.
Marcus But Dad, it's my room, and it's cool. Everybody does it.
Dad Yeah, everybody. I haven't got a black room.
Marcus You're not a teenager, and you're not cool.
Dad Thank God I'm not. You can paint it in blue.
Marcus Blue. How boring. Black or nothing.
Dad OK then, nothing it is. And now finish your breakfast. Time for school.
Marcus Can you drive me there?
Dad I don't know. Is that cool?

1 Marcus wants to paint his room. T / F
2 His dad says that he has to take off all his posters. T / F
3 Marcus wants 4 tins of black paint. T / F
4 His dad is against a black room. T / F
5 His dad thinks the room should be blue and green. T / F
6 Marcus only wants a black room. T / F
7 Marcus wants to go to school in his dad's car. T / F

★ **5 Read the beginning of Lemony Snicket's *The Bad Beginning*. Then add two or three sentences.**

If you are interested in stories with happy endings, you would be better off * reading some other book. In this book, not only is there no happy ending, there is no happy beginning and very few happy things in the middle. This is because not many happy things happened in the lives of the three Baudelaire youngsters*.

I would (not) like to read this book, because ...
....
....
....
....

Vocabulary:
*be better off – du solltest besser
youngster – Kind (umgangssprachlich)

▶ SB p. 135

★ **6 Read these two pages from Marcus's diary. Then answer the questions and give reasons.**

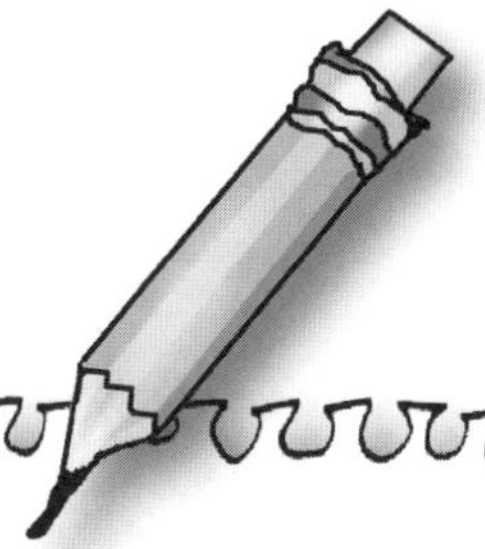

Saturday

First day of the holidays – and I'm in bed with a cold. I don't think it's the weather, it's the holidays. I need the school stress. No stress – and my body starts getting weak*. It wasn't a bad cold, but mum said, "Stay in bed for the weekend," and got me lots of DVDs (the Lemony Snicket film, too!), so it's OK. But in the afternoon Sam phoned. "We're all meeting in front of the shopping centre," he said. "Be there at six." I told him about my cold but he wasn't interested. "OK, then you won't see her." I asked him who "her" was, but he just laughed stupidly into the phone. After five minutes he finally said: "Jenny". Strange. I feel much better already. Two more hours to the meeting. Enough time to watch the Lemony Snicket DVD again.*

Sunday

Of course, yesterday was terrible. When I got to the shopping centre there were hundreds of kids there. OK, it was only 26 people, but still. Jenny was there, but she was holding hands with Matthew from 3C. I felt my cold coming back straightaway. Then it started raining and we all went to see the Fantastic Four. (I saw it two years ago, it's not really very good.) Matthew and Jenny were behind me. They didn't really watch the movie. I think they had a pretty good time. When I turned round and said "hush" a few times, Matthew hit me on the head. After the movie I went home. I was all wet from the rain when I got home. Now I've got a real cold. And I don't think Jenny is worth that. Have to think carefully about talking to Jenny next term. Maybe I'll punish* her and not talk to her.*

I also tore up the poem I wrote for her. (I never showed her the poem, of course.) I'm writing it down here to make sure I don't forget it. (And maybe I can use it for a girl called Penny or for another Jenny.)

Jenny, oh, Jenny
I think of you many
Times every day
Oh Jenny, I say
It is you that I miss.
Please give me a kiss.

1 Will he talk to Jenny next term?

....

....

2 Will he write another poem for her?

....

....

3 Will Marcus and Matthew still be best friends?

....

....

Vocabulary:
*cold – Erkältung
weak – schwach
movie – Film
punish – bestrafen

▶ SB p. **137**

Word File

MORE Words and Phrases

1	spot	*Some fish have spots on them.*	Fleck
	boot	*You'll need your boots to go walking.*	Stiefel
	diamond	*I'd love to have a diamond ring!*	Diamant
	toilet	*Excuse me, where's the toilet?*	Toilette, Klo
3	tell off	*If I'm late, the teacher will tell me off.*	ausschimpfen
	result	*As a result the student got told off.*	Folge; Ergebnis
	chess	*I think chess is better than sudoku.*	Schach(spiel)
	argument	*Don't start an argument.*	Wortwechsel; Streit
	smart	*She is very smart.*	schlau
	complicated	*It's a complicated problem. It'll take time to solve.*	kompliziert; schwierig
	track	*He ran twice around the track.*	Weg; Anlage
	unfortunately	*Unfortunately, I've forgotten where I put my mobile phone.*	unglücklicherweise
	go red	*I go red when girls talk to me.*	rot werden
	got to be …	*It's got to be blue.*	es muss (wohl) … sein
	shout out	*Then he shouted out my name.*	ausrufen
	read out	*He read out all the names of the best students.*	vorlesen
DVD	**I don't get it.**		Das versteh ich nicht.
	What for?		Wieso denn?

Show what you know Units 16–20

What I CAN DO in English

This page helps you to find out how well you are doing.
Read the statements and draw symbols.

☺ = I'm good at this ✓ = I can do this with help ☹ = I need to practise this more

Note:
Wenn du im Buch nachschauen willst, dann helfen dir die Seitenzahlen. Das zeigen sie dir an:

Words

- ◯ I can name at least 6 words and phrases about video games and virtual worlds. (16/110-112)
- ◯ I can name at least eight phrases for caring for a pet. (17/116)
- ◯ I can name at least 12 sports. (18/122)
- ◯ I can name at least eight weather conditions. (19/128)

Speaking

- ◯ I can talk about playing video games. (16/114)
- ◯ I can ask and answer questions about keeping a pet. (17/117)
- ◯ I can report answers from an interview to my class. (17/117)
- ◯ I can have a conversation about sports. (18/123)
- ◯ I can ask and answer questions with *Have you ever… ?*. (18/124)

Reading and listening

- ◯ I can read and understand dialogues about video or PC games. (16/110)
- ◯ I can listen to, read and understand the play *gamesworld.doc*. (16/111-112)
- ◯ I can listen to and understand what people say about video and PC games. (16/113)
- ◯ I can listen to and understand people talking about their pets. (17/117)
- ◯ I can listen to, read and understand the sketch *Small talk between dogs*. (17/118-119)
- ◯ I can read and understand the text *Where horses can live in peace*. (17/120)
- ◯ I can listen to and understand profiles of American teenagers. (18/123)
- ◯ I can read and understand profiles about people doing extreme sports. (18/125-126)
- ◯ I can listen to, read and understand weather forecasts. (19/129)
- ◯ I can listen to, read and understand conversations about the weather.
- ◯ I can read and understand texts about extreme weather conditions. (19/132)
- ◯ I can read, understand and answer questions in a quiz about my English book.
- ◯ I can read and understand somebody's diary for a week. (20/134-135)
- ◯ I can understand the words to the song *We're on holiday* and sing along. (20/138)

Writing for my Portfolio

- ◯ I have written a short text about a video game or why I (don't) like such games. (16/114)
- ◯ I have written a short text about a pet. (17/121)
- ◯ I have written a short text about sports. (18/127)
- ◯ I have written a holiday postcard to a friend. (19/132)

Acknowledgements

The publishers would like to thank the following for their kind permission to reproduce the following photographs and other copyright material:

Alamy p5, p47, p69, p112, p119; **Corbis** p7; **Helbling Languages** p89 (mobile phone; mp3; jeans); **©iStockphoto.com**/Jimak p4 /cjmckendry p77 /Liliboas /dkapp12 p95 (money; medicine); **Shutterstock EML**, Styve Reineck, John Bell p30, juza p47 (picnic), Styve Reineck, CJPhoto, Cory Cartwright p67, saied shahin kiya, Yuri Arcurs, Suzanne Tucker, Michelle D. Milliman, Gelpi, AndreyTTL, Roman Sigaev, Elnur, NGP Photo, Sandra Caldwell, Natalia Siverina p89, Rafael Martin-Gaitero, Rui Vale de Sousa, Margaret Stephenson, Valery Potapova p95, Joe Gough, Elena Blokhina, Anthony Gaudio p108, Teze p111, franck camhi p113, Aleix Ventayol FarrÃ©s p114.

Every effort has been made to trace the owners of any copyright material in this book. If notified, the publisher will be pleased to rectify any errors or omissions.